HOW TO ARGUE WITH A CONSERVATIVE

How to Argue
with a Conservative

Neil Staebler & Douglas Ross

Grossman Publishers
New York
1965

To Victor and Alice Ross
and Burnette, Liz, Mike, and Sally Staebler
for your patience in listening
to our political arguments
these many years.

Acknowledgments

The title of this book might well have been suggested by the correspondence in any one of a hundred Congressional offices. Instead, we are indebted to Victor Navasky, editor of *Monocle* magazine, who looked at a previous manuscript on the liberal record of the last thirty years (condensed in Chapter V) and proposed the format and title we have used.

We are likewise deeply indebted to Burnette Staebler for her encouragement, her perceptive criticism, and her editorial insistence on brevity, a virtue not always present in practitioners of politics. The publisher, Richard Grossman, and his editor, Peter Weinberg, have done much to keep the argument of the book meaningful.

Four members of the faculty of the University of Michigan have helped to provide perspective and have counseled us in various ways: Gerhard Weinberg, Professor of History; Sidney Fine, Professor of History; Samuel Eldersveld, Chairman of the Department of Political Science and former mayor of Ann Arbor; and William Haber, former Chairman of the Department of Economics and now Dean of the College of Literature, Science, and the Arts. However, they cannot be held accountable for either the conservative or the liberal positions as we have described them.

The liberal record, Chapter IV, owes much to the thoughtful and lively work of Roger Lowenstein on an earlier study. Kent Anderson, Joy Kaiser, Martin Katz, and Lorraine Saginaw contributed significantly to the research material from which the book was drawn. Special thanks goes to Albert Klyberg for his research and advice.

Congressman John Dingell of Michigan was a constant source of encouragement. His administrative assistant, Jeannette Cantwell; Ray Courage, administrative assistant in the Staebler office; and the other members of both staffs were helpful in many ways. Among the people who worked on the countless research items were Dale Arnold, Christopher Cohen, Susan Lesser, Susan Rice, Harold Wolman, and David Zimmerman.

This book seems to have generated more paperwork than is usual for one of its size, and we are grateful for the expert typing of Alice Mott, Nancy Feikens, and Bernice Poe.

Neil Staebler
Douglas Ross

Table of Contents

Liberal government and the freedom of the American people are incompatible. / Allowing Big Government to take over can only end with Big Brother telling you what to do. / The welfare state places the individual in economic serfdom by making him economically dependent on governmental whims. / Liberals are interested in men merely as creatures of mass society, not as unique human beings having various rights as individuals. / American businessmen are witnessing the loss of their freedom due to interference by government bureaucrats. / Wasteful government spending and the confiscatory income tax hobble individual liberty.

Those liberal cradle-to-the-grave security schemes weaken character and stifle individual initiative. / The "progressive" income tax kills individual and corporate incentive by punishing those who have the get-up-and-go to get something done. / Liberalism promotes conformity at the expense of individuality, forcing every one to the low-

est common denominator. / *Liberals see only the economic side of man and not his spiritual side.* / *They fail to take the whole man into account.* / *The result of three decades of the welfare state has been national moral decay.* / *Today Americans are a pampered, overfed lot. The rugged individual is a man of the past.*

3 Socialism, states' rights, and the Constitution 64

Since the reign of FDR began, America has been moving rapidly down the road to socialism. / *Liberal principles and programs are just a mask for socialist ideas.* / *"Government planning" and "government regulation" are just other names for state control and socialism.* / *Once the government gets its foot in the door somewhere, it's only a matter of time until it takes over that area completely.* / *Liberal disregard of the Constitution and denial of the rights of sovereign states have made federal control of the individual and the economy inevitable.*

4 Accomplishments of liberal government 104

The New Deal was a complete failure. If it hadn't been for World War II, people would still be standing in bread lines. / *Liberals fail to understand the laws of supply and demand. Their fiscal manipulations have served only to upset the functioning of the free market.* / *Deficit spending and a growing national debt are bankrupting the country.* / *Private enterprise has been crippled by regulation and harried by government competition.* / *Big Government and Big Labor together are destroying the small businessman.* / *Liberal giveaway programs have made the farm problem worse, not better.* / *The burgeoning federal bureaucracy is wasteful and inefficient, and is fast becoming uncontrollable.*

5 Foreign policy 149

America is losing the cold war because of our "no win" foreign policy. / *Yalta, Korea, and Cuba are good examples of American losses through liberal weakness and indecision.* / *Peaceful coexistence is impossible. It is nothing more than a piece of Red propaganda, swallowed hook, line, and sinker by gullible liberals.* / *Foreign aid is nothing but a multi-billion-dollar boondoggle, wasting the money of American taxpayers. Everyone knows you can't buy friends.* / *The United Nations is in the hands of an international gang of soft-headed neutralists who play right into Red hands.*

6   Naïve optimism, idealism and change (basic
    philosophy)   189

> *Liberals are too optimistic having a sadly misplaced faith that they can change the condition of man's existence. | Liberals meddle with peoples' lives. | Liberal policies damage society by disturbing normal human reactions. | Liberals are too idealistic and impractical. | Liberal goals are impossibly utopian. | How can liberals expect to preserve American principles while advocating radical change? | How can any one tell if this county is following the right course?*

Introduction to the discussion

The United States is a nation born of conflict and bred to contention. In the brief span of its history as an independent state it has suffered a major civil war, several minor rebellions, and a continuing series of moral crises. Today, on a broad spectrum of issues, people of many political hues participate in a continuous freewheeling debate over the proper social and political values, now and for the future.

Often political discussion seems quite futile. Proponents of different viewpoints seem to be able to achieve an almost metaphysical symbolism in their use of language—a language which is private almost to the point of being occult. Often what one hears in a face to face confrontation is two individuals busily engaged in the reinforcement of their own ideas through abstruse speculation, not by any means the meeting or even the clash of two minds in some form of tangible discussion.

Thus, meaningful debate among proponents of opposing political viewpoints is difficult, sometimes impossible—a desperate voyage into the semantics of the improbable. Why, then, argue at all? Perhaps because, as essentially optimistic people, liberals believe in man as a being capable of change and of being changed. Somehow they continue to hope that they will be able to reach their political adversaries on some ground that will enable them to see the liberal viewpoint in at least a slightly better light.

Sometimes, however, this is not possible. Two groups of people living within two distinct spheres of thought and values can often do little more than come into conflict—verbal or otherwise.

Still, argument directed to intellect rather than to emotion, dealing with specific issues rather than abstract values, can on most occasions be fruitful, and can offer a meeting ground for people for whom it would otherwise be difficult to find a sound basis for discussions.

It is with this type of argument that this book is concerned. The book deals in a simple and direct manner with conservative criticisms of our present mode of government and the point by point refutation of these conservative charges.

This book does not attempt to be a text in political philosophy nor a guide to contemporary economics and social psychology. It does, however, explain the economic rationale behind much of the often bewildering array of government programs and translate theory into down-to-earth dollars-and-cents terms, which provide the layman with a sound basis for discussion.

The book is divided into a series of discussions on specific liberal-conservative points of contention. First the conservative takes the floor; then the liberal replies.

Use the book as you would any other handbook. Seek in the Table of Contents the specific conservative charge in which you are interested. Read that section and additional material relevant to it. The authors hope the book will provide a solid ground for the liberal to stand on. It is up to the reader to make his stance a comfortable one.

HOW TO ARGUE WITH A CONSERVATIVE

1
Freedom and the role of the government

The argument between conservatives and liberals hinges on freedom. They agree on its basic importance, disagree in defining it, and disagree on what is happening to it in the United States.

Underlying the conservative's fear that we are in danger of losing our freedom is the great growth, in our lifetime, of government. "With the coming of the New Deal," the conservative says, "Big Government began creeping into the lives of the American people—destroying the independence of the farmer, stifling the initiative of the small businessman, killing the incentive of the great corporation, and giving the lazy, the shiftless, and the slothful the feeling that the United States government somehow owed them a living."

Bigness in government is not the only threat to freedom, the conservative feels. Along with growth we should fear the great recent increases in centralization, in collectivism, in paternalism. These, the conservative says, not only destroy individualism, weaken local government, and create a dependence upon the state, but carry also a far more ominous threat—the danger of totalitarianism. A people that loses its self-reliance and no longer cherishes freedom is in danger of going the route of other countries that have been swallowed by Communism and Fascism.

High taxes, in the conservative view, are another denial of freedom, since they interfere with the individual's basic rights of possession and use of his property.

To all this the liberal replies that theoretical definition is not enough. Agreeing with the conservative that to explore the concept of freedom should be a constant concern of all Americans, the liberal suggests that to accomplish this we must study the practical realization of freedom, and the ways in which government affects it. To determine how, in fact, we implement freedom and to detect when it is being infringed upon, requires a specific situation-by-situation approach.

The nub of the argument about freedom lies just here. The conservative, measuring present policy against the past, seeing the dangers in following uncharted paths, finds it difficult, if not impossible, to believe that today and tomorrow we can hold government within limits, maintain its responsiveness to public opinion, prevent it from crushing initiative, and protect the rights of minorities. The liberal, using the past as only one element in his decision, treating each situation in specific terms, believes we can maintain—even extend—our American liberties.

The following is a discussion of some of the theories, facts, and specific details in the liberal-conservative confrontation on the issues of freedom.

• *Liberal government and the freedom of the American people are incompatible.*

CONSERVATIVE: I am pleased that we finally found an evening to consider the record of government over the past three decades and the legitimacy of the liberal's claim to the future. The liberal view of the proper role of government, based on statements liberals have offered, logically eliminates the possibility of achieving the maximum amount of freedom and, on the contrary, points toward totalitarianism.

For a start, a definition of "freedom" should be made. Quite simply, "freedom" is that condition in which men confront no obstacles to the realization of their desires. Obviously, no one ever enjoys absolute freedom; physical and psychological limitations as well as the conflicting desires of various members of society will always prevent people from fulfilling their every wish. The question, one that members of every society should repeatedly ask themselves, is therefore one of degree. By what means can the greatest possible degree of freedom be achieved while, at the same time, the proper balance between the rights of every individual is maintained?

An insight into the conservative approach to this problem can be found in a key passage of Barry Goldwater's *The Conscience of a Conservative:*

> Throughout history, government has proved to be the chief instrument for thwarting man's liberty. Government represents power in the hands of some men to control and regulate the lives of other men. And power, as Lord Acton said, corrupts men. "Absolute Power," he added, "corrupts absolutely."

I wish to explain the significance of this passage very carefully, because liberals have a tendency to oversimplify and distort the conservative position. In the first place, it doesn't mean that we flatly hold that "the government that governs least governs best." This is an anarchistic sentiment. Conservatives have always recognized that the practice of freedom requires the establishment of order. However, the power of the state need not restrict freedom at all. The four legitimate functions of government—the preservation of internal order, the provision of a defense against foreign enemies, the administration of justice, and the maintenance of competition and the free interchange of goods—serve to allow the individual the maximum amount of freedom to follow his chosen pursuits by removing those factors which could restrict him. What Senator Goldwater was saying is that to permit the men who wield the power of government to transgress these legitimate limits of activity is to court disaster. Political power has an insatiable appetite which, if not checked, will consume the individual's power and consequently his freedom.

Compare this concept of limited government intervention in the defense of freedom with the liberal approach. Liberals of both political parties readily admit that when a job needs doing and no one else is willing or able to do it, this job automatically becomes the proper function of the federal government. However, if one allows government to expand its jurisdiction and intervene in areas beyond the legitimate limits I have just stated, it follows that, as a result, individual freedom will necessarily be diminished. Specifically what I mean is that when a government is carrying out properly the four functions that I previously enumerated, that government is acting in such a manner as to allow the maximum amount of freedom. To allow government to extend its power beyond these stated limits can only create obstacles to freedom.

Perhaps a few specific examples will help make things clearer. When the firms that comprise a particular industry work in collusion to keep wages low, free competition for the services of labor is impeded and the individual worker's freedom to reserve his services for the highest bidder is destroyed. Under these circumstances, it is quite proper for the government to remove this obstacle to the worker's freedom by prohibiting this anticompetitive practice. However, if the government refuses to stop at this point of maximum freedom and goes on to enact minimum-wage and maximum-hour laws, individual freedom is again restricted; for, now government is obstructing the determination of wages in the market place, the very process which it had initially intervened to preserve. It is precisely this kind of contradictory behavior which has been depriving us of our liberty during the past three decades. Social security, which denies every American the right to spend and save his income when and as he pleases, is another instance of this tragic liberal transgression. The essential point to bear in mind is that this loss of liberty is not the work of evil men, but the unavoidable result of the liberal attitude toward government.

Furthermore, the liberal belief in the right of government to do whatever needs doing is completely at odds with the primary purpose of the Constitution—the preservation of limited government in America. Washington, Jefferson, Franklin, and all of the other statesmen who created our governmental system recognized a fundamental law of history which liberals seem to have missed: Release the holders of state power from any restraints other than those they wish to impose upon themselves, and you are swinging down the well-traveled road to absolutism. It should be obvious that the concentration of unlimited power in the hands of the state leaves the people with no power and, consequently, with no freedom beyond that which the government chooses to grant them.

LIBERAL: You believe that this is what liberals favor?

CONSERVATIVE: Maybe not consciously; but where else can a government lead which is instructed to decide for itself what it should undertake, with absolutely no regard for the Constitution and its explicit definition of the rightful duties of government?

You might argue that civic-spirited public officials are not interested in creating a totalitarian state; but you would be ignoring the inescapable fact that men with some power usually want more. If they tell themselves that they need the additional power to improve the well-being of the nation, I have no reason to doubt their sincerity. However, the benevolence of a dictatorship doesn't alter the basic fact that such a government *is* a dictatorship in which the individual's freedom is no longer secure.

All you have to do is take a look at the federal government today to realize that such a centralization of power is already well advanced in this country. A study by a leading newspaper recently revealed that the federal government is currently the biggest landowner, property manager, renter, mover and hauler, medical clinician, lender, insurer, mortgage broker, employer, debtor, taxer, and spender in all history. Since the election of President Franklin Roosevelt, the executive and judicial branches of the government have been wandering further and further beyond the constitutionally-prescribed bounds of their responsibilities, while Congress, the most representative branch, has been relegated to the secondary role of rubber stamp for the president's policies and programs. Each successive liberal step toward utopia—the New Deal, the Fair Deal, the New Frontier, and the Great Society—has witnessed an increased outpouring of legislation, and nearly every act has erected an additional obstacle to freedom.

Whenever I point this out to liberals, they usually try to explain away this tremendous centralization of power by claiming that it reflects "the will of the people." This somewhat specious rationalization was anticipated by Alexis de Tocqueville, that remarkable Frenchman who visited this country in the 1830's. De Tocqueville wrote that he feared that Americans would some day default their freedom to their government and then "console themselves for being in tutelage by the reflection that they have chosen their own guardians. Every man allows himself to be put in lead strings, because he sees that it is not a person nor a class of persons, but the people at large that hold the end of his chain." My answer is that if the end result is a society without freedom, it makes little difference whether the people voted away their liberty or whether it was seized by tyrants; the people are in bondage regardless of the name they give their master.

So, if you will concede that no government with a political philosophy which necessarily diminishes individual freedom instead of increasing it should be acceptable to the American people, we can avoid entering into a dragged-out discussion about deficit spending, defense strategy, and the like. I say that liberalism is such a philosophy, and that liberal government, which has already destroyed much of our freedom over the past third of a century, is sure to finish the job in the future. Unless you can come up with some good counterarguments, this discussion is almost over.

LIBERAL: You will be surprised to know that I agree with much of what you say, although I hope that I can find enough holes in your argument to prevent it from putting a quick end to this long-awaited discussion.

To start with, I accept both your definition of freedom as the absence of obstacles to the realization of desires and your designation of freedom as the primary goal of every American government, past, present, and future. Liberals have always regarded the maximization of the individual's power to accomplish what he wants as the paramount function and obligation of government. But I would like to take a look at a few of your conclusions.

I am afraid I couldn't follow the logic of your contention that any exercise of governmental power in excess of the four tasks you enumerated *necessarily* entails a loss of individual freedom. You are proposing an abstract discussion of a problem which, by its very nature, depends on an understanding of the specific facts in each situation. So, before we go on with this discussion of government intervention and individual liberty, I suggest that an examination of individual situations would be far more fruitful, and that this should be done before you attempt to draw any general conclusions.

Your claim that the police power of the state promotes individual freedom by forcing everyone to observe certain regulations for preserving public order is no more or less compelling than the claim that freedom is increased when workers are forced to contribute a portion of their earnings to a social-security fund. In theory, both enforcements can either remove barriers to the individual's ability to fulfill his desires or erect new ones. If internal order is maintained by means of a secret police force with the power to arrest and search at will, individuals sacrifice more freedom than they gain. Likewise, a social-insurance program that stipulates how recipients must spend their benefits creates more obstacles to freedom than it eliminates.

All that we can conclude *a priori* is that government intervention will eliminate some freedom somewhere. The very act of intervening insures that certain alternatives will be prohibited, even if it is only the freedom to beat one's wife. The meaningful question is: Will the gain in freedom outweigh the losses? This question cannot be answered safely on the basis of universals about power or human nature, but only by examining each situation as it arises. As Harry Girvetz points out in *The Evolution of Liberalism:*

> In the end, there is only one test by which to determine an excess or a defect of power: does it resolve the needs which called it into being in such a way as to promote human freedom? If power is greater than the situation calls for, it is tyrannical. But if it is less, and this is what is often forgotten, the final result will also be tyranny.

CONSERVATIVE: You mean to say you can't discern a significant difference either in theory or in practice between a government that employs its police power to keep people from taking what isn't theirs and a government that enacts a social-security scheme which confiscates what rightfully does belong to people?

LIBERAL: Of course police power and social insurance represent different kinds of government intervention, both in theory *and* in practice. All I am attempting to establish is the impossibility of determining how either of these dissimilar uses of state power will affect freedom without knowing the particulars of their implementation.

Let me give you an example. Sixty years ago, downtown traffic was a matter of a few horse-and-buggy rigs. The need for

regulation was minimal, so there was no real question of government intervention. But as the automobile became more popular,
both the density and speed of traffic increased to the point where
it became necessary for the city to intervene in order to prevent
chaos and congestion, to say nothing of danger to human life.
Think of the carnage that would have resulted, if people had
been allowed to set their individual standards of speed and
safety.

Now, when the automobile is pretty much a standard part of
our life, traffic regulations have been further tightened with one-
way streets, parking regulations, special turn signals, and a
whole variety of fairly complex procedures—all of which further
restrict the motorist from being able to decide what he wishes
to do.

Sure, a good deal of freedom has been lost by the motorist;
but, without this loss, driving conditions would be so bad that
the question of freedom would scarcely be relevant. On one
hand, the driver has lost the freedom to negotiate intersections
completely as he wishes to; but, on the other hand, he has gained
a certain confidence that he will be able to reach his destination,
a situation which would hardly be possible today without traffic
regulation. Thus, in exchange for a certain loss of freedom by
traffic regulation, the driver has gained a greater freedom to get
where he wants.

This is not to say that every possible traffic control would
have the effect of expanding the motorist's freedom. If the city
council decided that congestion could best be relieved by limiting each car owner to two hours of driving a day, I, for one,
would protest that this governmental power was disproportion-
ate to the problem at hand. We would be sacrificing far too
much for the extra safety that would result. In this particular
instance, after weighing all factors, we would conclude that government intervention had lessened our liberty.

This brings me back to my original point: With the traffic
problem, as with any other situation which may arise, there is no
way of determining whether granting the government additional

power will increase freedom or promote absolutism unless we are acquainted both with the specific government power being exercised and with the problem in question. If, as you say, a third of a century of liberal government has robbed us of much of our liberty, this conclusion can only be reached by examining the effects of liberal programs, not by means of abstract proofs.

However, for the purposes of argument, assume that in theory your list of four legitimate governmental functions does allow the greatest amount of individual freedom; that a government which protects the governed against a breakdown of public order, against foreign invasion, against illegal activity, and against the unlawful restraint of commerce ought to leave the individual with the greatest possible liberty to live his life as he chooses. That is the theory. To test it in practice we must now ask: Do individuals actually possess the opportunities and abilities to take advantage of these conditions of freedom?

Tell a Negro that he is free to join certain trade unions because there are no laws that forbid it and he'll laugh in your face; he knows that prejudice has robbed him of that opportunity. A middle-aged man who has just lost his assembly-line job because of automation is not barred from finding another job by any law; but he will probably remain unemployed all the same. His freedom to locate a new job is meaningless if he lacks the requisite training and encounters age discrimination. Most seventeen-year-old high school dropouts are not free to do anything except hang around street corners and get into trouble unless they receive further training and counseling.

Liberals believe that liberty demands that government play a dual role. The essentially negative application of government power—enforcement of basic laws and removal of unnecessary restraints—must be supplemented with a more positive type of intervention aimed at enabling people to realize the freedom that your four "proper" functions of state have made available. Only after your abstract idea of freedom has been translated into an attainable everyday reality can we talk of a society with a maximum of freedom for all individuals.

Yes, we do entertain different ideas about the proper limits of government activity. You believe that the state need only open the door to freedom to fulfill its purpose, while I contend that the government's responsibility doesn't end until it has helped the governed obtain the opportunities and abilities to walk through that door.

CONSERVATIVE: And so government keeps interfering with our lives until every one everywhere in America lives on easy street, regardless of how hard he has or hasn't worked to get there.

LIBERAL: Not quite. I think your estimate is a bit high. Most liberals would be happy to see that day when all willing and able men and women in this country can find jobs which provide them with a decent standard of living. As long as individuals encounter obstacles to the achievement of their goals, liberals believe that government must remain available as *one* of a number of possible devices of liberation.

But let me return to the question of how we judge the relation of government and freedom. Up to now, all I have tried to demonstrate is that government intervention doesn't *necessarily* diminish freedom. If a government's function is to preserve and extend freedom, we defeat its purpose when we allow it to remove legal restraints to liberty while forbidding it to deal with the social and economic forces that often compromise men's goals. What all this means is that the only fair way to discuss the results of the past three decades is in terms of the specific accomplishments of liberalism.

Obviously we haven't time to run through every measure Congress has enacted since 1933. So let's analyze a representative liberal program that you have singled out: the social-security system. As I conceded earlier, compulsory social insurance entails the loss of one very real freedom: the freedom to spend as we wish the amounts deducted from every pay check to finance the program. On the opposite side of the ledger, we obtain the freedom from extreme deprivation in times of unemployment and old age. Unfortunately, no one has yet discovered any quantitative measure, such as the *utile* or *erg,* with which to determine objectively whether the freedom gained is greater than the freedom given up. If most individuals believe that the freedom from want is worth more than the freedom to spend social-security deductions, they will elect legislators pledged to establish a social-insurance plan; and if, after a while, the majority decides they don't like it, they can institute procedures for the program's repeal.

CONSERVATIVE: Wait just a minute. Think about what you've just said. You are supporting the right of government to increase the freedom of some at the expense of the freedom of others. "Tyranny of the majority" describes a situation in which a majority, no matter how narrow, is allowed to force its will upon the millions who, in the case of social security, may regard the freedom to plan privately for their old age more highly than the acquisition of a public insurance policy. If you were honestly interested in maximizing the freedom of every individual, you would favor the conservative proposal to make social security voluntary. Then you could have your insurance and I could enjoy my freedom from it. Doesn't that make a lot more sense?

LIBERAL: With some programs it might, but not with social security. The underlying principle of public insurance is to spread the risk over an entire population in order to make individual coverage inexpensive enough for everyone to afford. Certain programs must be mandatory in order to work. Next time you get stopped for speeding, tell the officer that you have decided that the freedom to drive as fast as you want is personally worth more to you than the additional freedom from accidents you obtain by staying below the limit; the ticket he issues you is society's judgment that in order to be effective for any, speed limits must be adhered to by all. Social security is a similar case.

Are these both instances of a tyranny of the majority? Admittedly, the line between the legitimate will of the majority and the

violation of the rights of the minority is a fine one. If a representative system is to function, the majority must be able to implement its decisions—unless, that is, these decisions deprive some
individuals of certain basic rights. When fundamental liberties
like freedom of speech or the opportunity to earn a decent living
are abrogated, the democratic process has indeed degenerated
into a tyranny of the few by the many. But compelling people
to delay spending eight percent of their annual incomes up to
$6,600 until a later day and enforcing speed limits hardly seem
to fall into this category.

If you took the time to repeat this evaluative procedure with
each federal action since FDR's inauguration thirty-some years
ago, I am confident that, on the whole, you would discover that
the freedoms which liberal government has destroyed have been
replaced by what most Americans hold to be greater freedoms.
Of course, there have been exceptions: the National Industrial
Recovery Act, drafted in the depths of the Depression, granted
the government considerable power over business, and, in my
opinion, it was rightly condemned by the Supreme Court as unconstitutional. But these exceptions have remained few and far
between.

CONSERVATIVE: Even if we assume that these liberal activities
have had the initial effect of expanding freedom, if they bring
about a government which we can't control, hasn't the price of
this extra freedom been too high?

LIBERAL: It has indeed. But, I don't agree with your implica-
tion that liberal government and limited government are incompatible. All you have to do is spend a few days on Capitol Hill to
be convinced that this isn't the case.

In the first place, liberals have never thought that the proper
realm of federal activity is what federal officials arbitrarily decide it will be; the Constitution designates definite limitations as
does the liberal philosophy. But even if liberals believed pro-
foundly that the government should do whatever the president

and his friends in Congress want done, what makes you think they could get away with it?

All of the checks and balances designed by the founding fathers to keep the federal government representative and responsive to the people's wishes are still operative, and many have been improved and expanded over the years. The greatest power the citizen has over his government is the right to vote it in or out of office. This right was restricted to white, male property owners 175 years ago; today it is the legal right, though not always the actual one, of every American of voting age, regardless of race, sex, or economic condition. Whereas senators used to be appointed by their respective state legislatures, they are presently chosen directly by the people. The existence of opposing political parties, numerous lobbies, well-financed special-interest groups, and improved mass communications provide more assurance than ever that all voices will be heard. Every appropriation bill in Congress must still be voted up to eighteen different times before it becomes law. And, if you believe that Congress has become so subservient to the president, how do you explain the fact that Truman, Eisenhower, and Kennedy experienced so little success in getting even a part of their programs passed? I could go on and on, because Americans of the 1960's have far more power to limit their government's actions than they have ever had.

As for Monsieur de Tocqueville's reminder that a people can vote away their liberty as well as have it seized from them, it is a warning worth repeating often. But having made citizens aware of this danger, we can only hope that the majority is sufficiently informed and politically sophisticated to distinguish between what will promote its freedom and what will diminish it. Although I don't often agree with Barry Goldwater, like him I am convinced that the individual is able to recognize what serves his own interests best. This sustains my belief—which I'm not sure he shares—that we *will* manage as a nation to hold on to our liberty.

When everything has been said, there is no escaping the fact that you and I define the proper uses of government power quite differently. Liberals are aware of the potential threat to freedom that the state poses. But they also realize that, given adequate democratic checks and controls, limited government power is a valuable tool with which to modify or eliminate the many social and economic forces which keep men from living as they wish. The goal of contemporary liberalism is not a political order in which freedom is diminished, but rather a society in which all individuals actually experience the liberty which is guaranteed them in the Constitution. As I see it, not only is the theory of liberal government consistent with the preservation and expansion of individual freedom, but in practice, it has been increasing our freedoms for a third of a century.

• *Allowing Big Government to take over can only end with Big Brother telling you what to do.*

CONSERVATIVE: Your counter to my charge that the liberal view of government must inevitably lead to a loss of individual freedom contains one glaring weakness. Your so-called "positive" government may or may not increase individual freedom at the outset, but it must, by definition, bring about a centralization of power; and, historically, the concentration of power in the state has nearly always ended in totalitarianism. So you've generated a very revealing paradox: The more government intervenes in an effort to liberate the individual, the closer society moves to a state of absolutism in which alternatives and choice are eliminated and freedom is destroyed.

Again and again the past has reminded us that increased government power is a prelude to the passing of freedom. The men who wrote the Constitution were well aware of this. This is why they sought to commit America to a course which liberals have cavalierly abandoned.

And there is no excuse for your failure to recognize where

liberal philosophy is taking us. For the past half century, we've been almost continually at war with totalitarian systems in which people have defaulted all power to the state in return for the promise of a better life or greater national glory. Look at Nazi Germany, Fascist Italy, and Communist Russia. Yet, despite all of this evidence, liberals are always requesting just a little more power for the state in order to enhance our "welfare": First, the federal government must intervene to vanquish poverty once and for all; next they call on Washington to protect civil rights—an area already within the purview of the states; someday there'll be the pressing demand for government owned transportation and so the list runs on endlessly into the future.

In their haste to project a progressive, modern image, liberals have forgotten that an understanding of the present requires an acquaintance with the past. This tragic oversight might well cost us our freedom if it isn't corrected.

LIBERAL: I agree that we must understand what has come before to obtain the broadest possible perspective of the present and future. But, we have to be careful not to generalize about events of today from the particulars of the past. And we should avoid misinterpreting the cause of former events, in our eagerness to have them support our interpretation of what has happened in the recent past or what could happen in the near future.

As you explained, the colonists' fear of central government was no mystery, given the world in which they lived. During the formative years of this nation, most European governments were unrepresentative. They tended to intervene in the economic and social activities of their peoples in an arbitrary, repressive fashion, which was rarely in the interests of the great majority of the governed, who, for the most part, were legally excluded from political participation. Even England, whose constitutionalism had such a significant impact on the development of our own civil institutions, was ruled by tight aristocratic cliques. Throughout Europe the middle class, despite its growing financial power, found itself balked by the old order which, through the mechanisms of state, worked to protect the privileged position of an established minority. In short, central government was said to be the greatest threat to liberty in the eighteenth century and much of the nineteenth century because its past behavior had warranted such a judgment; an increase in the state's power was almost always accompanied by a corresponding decrease in individual freedom.

But to reach universal conclusions from the fact that a centralization of government power can and often has led to the loss of freedom attributes to history a determinism it doesn't deserve. In doing so, you are ignoring important qualitative differences between governments, such as their responsiveness to constituent wishes and needs, the means by which they were selected, the processes and procedures by which they must abide, their past performances, and their plans for the future. Surely you wouldn't entrust your "legitimate" functions of government, such as the power to maintain internal order, to a state headed by a Louis XV or a Hitler. In debating the proper scope of government activity, though we disagree over boundary lines, we were both assuming a responsive representative government of the type we enjoy in this country—a type of broadly-based representative democracy which, I might add, has no precedent in earlier periods. Therefore, any attempt to apply to the western democracies of the 1960's the arguments against the despotisms of the past is an anachronism and not very relevant to our current concern with liberty.

Your effort to link liberal interventionism and totalitarianism is more pertinent, but it simply isn't substantiated by what has happened. Name one liberal government in the twentieth century which has transformed itself into a totalitarian regime by means of a steady centralization of power. There have not been any.

Germany's liberal experiment after World War I didn't culminate in Hitler's Nazi dictatorship because of gradually expanded government intervention. On the contrary, the collapse of the Weimar Republic was more likely the consequence of its inability to solve the problem of mass instability which plagued that country. Liberal democracy was discredited on the Rhine, it seems to me, not because the government tried to gather or succeeded in accumulating too much power unto itself, but because the German people's inability to agree on fundamental social aims condemned the government to inaction. In Germany the democratic government came to stand for stalemate and paralysis. It was as a result of this political and governmental vacuum that Hitler's promise to put the country on its feet again was heeded by the German people. In Italy, much the same thing occurred.

With Russia, China, and certain Eastern European and Asian countries it wasn't a question of democratic failure, but rather of Communist totalitarianism directly replacing more primitive royal, aristocratic, and military absolutisms. The people of these nations did not barter their freedom for "bread and circuses"— they had never had such freedom to lose.

If there is any lesson to be drawn from recent history concerning the use or abuse of democratic power, it might well be that to prevent a democracy from coping with the problems of its citizens is the surest way to seal its doom and promote the possibility of a totalitarian successor. In other words government power that is too limited can be just as dangerous as government power that is unlimited.

• *The welfare state places the individual in political serfdom by making him economically dependent on government.*

CONSERVATIVE: You still do not see the contradiction inherent in your liberal concept of "positive" government. Maybe an example from my own experience will help clarify my point.

When I was a child our household was run as a dictatorship with my father as autocrat in residence. He told me when to go to sleep, when to get up, when to study, and when to brush my teeth—all of which was becoming somewhat embarrassing by the time I reached the age of seventeen. The source of his control, aside from the fact that he was legally my father, derived from my total dependence on him for my material wants. As the provider of my sustenance, he maintained the right to regulate all of my affairs, economic and noneconomic alike; and, short of running away from home, there wasn't a thing I could do about it.

Now paternalism and the power to enforce it are expected and probably even required of parents, who can usually be counted on to end it when the youth attains his majority. But when government assumes this same role, it means the permanent loss of freedom for everyone.

The liberal welfare state may not yet match Orwell's description of 1984, but it is well on its way. Several million Americans already depend directly on the federal government for the necessities of life. Every person who receives social-security retirement benefits, federal food stamps, aid-to-dependent-children payments, War-on-Poverty wages, federal pay checks, or outright welfare turns over to government the responsibility of caring for his essential personal needs—in some cases from the cradle to the grave. And, just as my material reliance on my father made me subject to his will, welfarism puts the individual at the mercy of the state. "The State that is able to deal with its citizens as wards and dependents," Barry Goldwater correctly observed, "has gathered unto itself unlimited political and economic power and is thus able to rule as absolutely as any oriental despot."

It is that simple. When a people permit a government to supply them with complete economic security by means of welfare schemes and handouts, they have conceded to that government the ultimate political power—the power to extend or withhold the means of human subsistence as the government sees fit. Under these conditions, individual freedom ceases to exist.

This is the contradiction inherent in the welfare state. By giving the government the power to guarantee the individual's economic security, you necessarily destroy all those guarantees to his liberty which you claim to be strengthening; for, economic dependence and political independence are incompatible.

1984 is less than twenty years away, and I'm afraid we'll arrive there right on schedule if liberals are left in Washington much longer.

LIBERAL: Before I can do much to allay your fears for our future, I think we ought to discuss this concept of "welfarism" to which you keep referring. I have no objection to using "welfare state" as a synonym for liberal government if you wish; but if we are going to use it, we should determine what it signifies within the context of contemporary American liberalism.

Your representation of the welfare state in America conjures up images of the consuls of imperial Rome distributing grain to the starving plebeians in return for their promise of good behavior and political acquiescence. How this resembles the operations of our government is hard to understand.

In the United States, fifty-seven percent of all federal government payments to individuals—the type you have characterized as "welfare" payments—take the form of benefits from prepaid public insurance policies. These policies don't render the recipient any more dependent on the state than a commercial retirement plan would put one at the mercy of the president and board of the Prudential Life Insurance Company. Collecting my social-security checks when I reach the age of sixty-five will not involve going to some government official to plead my case and maybe bartering my vote in return for his sympathetic consideration; my benefits are guaranteed by law and determined by the amount that I have contributed to the social-security fund during my working years.

Money received through the various programs that comprise our social-insurance system is no different than that which is received through private plans, except that the government serves as the actuarial agent instead of a private concern. With social insurance, the benevolence and discretion of the state are never allowed to enter into the picture. I really don't see how this kind of "welfare" payment could compromise my political and economic independence in the slightest. No government could successfully employ the threat of withholding these payments as a means of subordinating the individual to the state as long as our democratic devices for limiting government remained in working order. If such an attempt were made today, we would promptly vote the malefactors out of power. In other words, the conversion of our social-insurance system into a weapon for political coercion could only be the *result* of a totalitarian system, and never its cause.

This leaves the forty-three percent of federal welfare expenditures which are used to finance noninsurance benefits to be accounted for. Of this amount, two-fifths goes for education, vocational rehabilitation, and health services, all of which are administered on the state and local level. None of these provide any government, much less the federal government, with the opportunity to deny the needy the necessities of life. Another two-fifths is used in the numerous veterans' programs which have been authorized by both conservative and liberal Congresses ever since the Revolutionary War. These programs are not considered to be welfare payments in the conventional sense, but rewards for bearing arms in defense of the country, unrelated to the veteran's economic situation.

The remaining fifth—a sum about half as large as the annual appropriation of federal grants for highway construction—is spent for what is called "public aid." This welfare category provides assistance to the aged poor and sick, to dependent children, to the blind, and to the long-term totally disabled. I think these must have been the type of programs you had in mind when you spoke of individuals becoming economically dependent on the government, because many of those receiving these public-aid payments rely on them as their sole means of support. But any dependence involved is not subject to federal exploitation or control. Every one of these programs is administered by state and local officials who make all the discretionary decisions permitted under the law. The federal government is limited to supplying roughly fifty percent of the required funds and to designating certain minimum standards, which doesn't even keep regulations and procedures from varying between states and often from county to county.

CONSERVATIVE: But what about the several million able-bodied Americans who live on welfare simply because they find it easier than working? You neglected to include them.

LIBERAL: For once you have asked me a question that I wanted to hear. The concept of a general federal dole is a myth! Federal relief for the poor who do not fall into one of the special categories listed under public aid simply doesn't exist. When you talk about the "able-bodied poor" going downtown every week to pick up their welfare checks, you're referring to state, county, and local relief programs which receive no federal money and are subject to no federal authority. The War on Poverty, though locally run, *does* pay out federal money to the employable poor in the form of wages for education and job training that will increase the receiver's economic independence and hopefully get him off the welfare rolls. But this can hardy be called a dole; "investment" would be a more accurate description.

So I am perfectly willing to use the term "welfare state" to denote liberal government in this country, as long as we remember that "welfare state" in this context describes a federal government which dispenses nearly sixty percent of its social welfare benefits in the form of insurance payments, and the rest— with the exception of the veterans' benefits—through programs administered and partially financed by state and local institutions; a government, in short, whose objective is not the material subservience of the individual, but the economic self-sufficiency of every person with the age, health, and potential ability to earn a decent living.

I will accept your statement that total economic dependence and political independence are difficult to maintain simultaneously; but what I want to know is: Who are these Americans whom you claim have become the "wards" of the federal government? The only major noninsurance program of federal welfare payments exclusively supervised and funded by the national government is that established for veterans, and most of our ex-soldiers do not rely on these federal checks for their day-to-day existence. Therefore, unless you can point out this dependent mass of humanity you mentioned to me, I see no reason to place any special significance to the coming of 1984.

• *Liberals are interested in men merely as creatures of mass society, not as unique human beings having various rights as individuals.*

CONSERVATIVE: You accepted my definition of freedom as the absence of restraints to the fulfillment of individual desires. How, then, given the diverse desires of 200 million Americans, can liberals claim that they are maximizing individual freedom with welfare schemes which supply only collective answers to our problems? After all, what frees one man may restrict another if they have different ends in mind. Compulsory social insurance will help one accomplish what he wants if economic security is one of his goals; but if he values a current high standard of living more than increased protection in his old age, the Social Security Act of 1935 places a very formidable obstacle in his path.

By enacting such laws, liberals have taken it upon themselves to prescribe what values and priorities every individual "ought" to hold, assuming that one "ought" to prefer security when he is ninety-three years old to a bigger house today. Liberal effort to subordinate individual choice to the "collective will" or, more accurately, to the state's judgment of what is best for every one contradicts everything the conservative stands for. We recognize that each man is unique, and since only he can fully know what he wants from life, to allow any other human being or collectivity of human beings to make the decisions that shape his destiny cannot possibly maximize his freedom. This can only be done by making him responsible for his own development and seeing to it that he encounters a minimum of interference.

In short, liberals are guilty of two fundamental errors, one of logic and the other of ego. They assume that collective action can increase the freedom of all individuals, no matter how conflicting their desires. Further, they claim an omniscience which they seem to think gives them the right to tell the rest of us how to conduct our affairs. As for this last bit of self-delusion, I can only join with Barry Goldwater in declaring that the true conservative will always stand opposed not only to dictators who rule by terror, but to "those gentler collectivists who ask our permission to play God with the human race."

LIBERAL: Liberals have never endorsed collective action as a panacea for all of mankind's problems. We have always believed that most aspects of life are peculiar to the individual and should be subject solely to his control. But people's individual differences do not prevent them from pursuing common ends or from encountering common barriers in the pursuit of different ends. In these circumstances, freedom may require social organization or cooperative effort.

When you stated earlier that law enforcement represents one of the legitimate functions of government, you were saying much the same thing; individuals trying to realize various desires can be blocked by a common barrier—in this instance, criminal activity—which can best be removed through collective action. The big difference between liberals and conservatives on this issue is that liberals think that this sound line of reasoning should be extended to include nonlegal barriers as well.

The increasingly critical problem of water pollution is a good case in point. Industrialists, commercial fishermen, sportsmen, and housewives regard our water supply with dissimilar intentions. But whether they view water primarily as an element in a manufacturing process, as a direct source of livelihood, as a means of recreation, or as something to wash the children's clothes in, they will all be prevented from doing what they want if the water is dirty. To instruct an irate mother who is demanding pure drinking water for her children to go down to the river with her sieve and shovel and clean up the water makes as much sense as telling her to learn judo and carry a gun if she wants to be safe on the streets. The only way to abate pollution is through the cooperation of the entire community; and, since government is supposedly the people organized in order to accomplish what they can't do singly or in private groups, government is the instrument for the job. Local and state governments should do all they can, and when the pollution cuts across state lines, the federal government must also play a part. If government succeeds in solving the problem, you have a good example of collective action increasing the freedom of individuals with very different goals.

Of course such cooperative efforts will restrict some individuals more than others. Police regulations hit the criminal hardest just as water pollution controls hamper the polluter most; all of which takes us back to our earlier discussion of the rights of the majority in a democratic society. If most individuals feel that their liberty to achieve their own objectives will be promoted by a given government intervention, they must be permitted to implement their will, provided that certain fundamental rights of those who oppose the action are respected. The alternative of letting the few block the many is certainly a strange formula for maximizing freedom.

You mentioned social security. This is a case where people with different values and aspirations share a common goal—an income to support themselves in their old age. Qualifying for benefits requires only that an individual has worked an equivalent of ten years before retirement, and there are no stipulations limiting the recipient's use of his checks. He can bury them in the back yard, drink them up at the local bar, or depend on them as his means of support. In passing the Social Security Act in 1935, Congress wasn't "prescribing" what the people "ought" to believe about the alternative of having either protection against material want tomorrow or a larger house today. The act reflected the opinion of most congressmen that a majority of people wanted such a plan. If they had misjudged the wishes of the majority, the voters would have told them about it in the elections the following fall. As for the freedom of those who opposed this program of compulsory saving, our national legislators felt that the small percentage of income deducted from each pay check to finance the program would not significantly alter the standard of living of those who preferred to spend all their earnings immediately.

CONSERVATIVE: Your argument might have possessed some weight thirty years ago when social-security deductions totaled two percent of every pay check. However, today they account for nearly ten percent of every dollar earned, and there is nothing to keep them from climbing to fifteen percent, twenty percent, or who knows what. You're bound to reach a point, if you haven't hit it already, at which the minority's right to live as they wish will be destroyed. How will you justify your collective scheme when that happens?

LIBERAL: If there does come a time when the carrying out of the social-security program unreasonably punishes those who oppose its existence, the particular extensions of the program which pushed it to that point will receive my vigorous opposition as well as yours. Unfortunately, there is no specific cut-off point of "x" percent that can be designated in advance as an unreasonable amount for social-security deductions. We can only judge what seems best for the present and the very near future; we cannot look much farther ahead. If the burden of social security becomes too great, enough people will complain about it to cause the government to take measures to remedy the situation.

CONSERVATIVE: What makes you think the government would respond if the minority did protest?

LIBERAL: You keep implying that the government and the governed are two mutually-exclusive entities locked in a liberty-or-slavery struggle for supremacy. The government in this country is merely an extension of the people, and the people possess the power to change its structure and personnel as they please.

When a minority of the people is harmed by a majority enactment, this minority is free to publicize its grievance. If the minority is successful in getting a majority to support its views, the government has no choice but to redress the situation or be defeated at the polls. The civil rights movement has demonstrated that the opportunity to transform a minority into a majority is more than theoretical. After a century of acquiescence the Negro found a voice to tell of the degradation of a white-imposed second-class citizenship. Gradually, much of America has come to realize the justice of the Negro's cause. The result has been a series of federal, state, and local actions to help correct this terrible wrong. As long as freedom of expression is preserved and democratic processes insure a responsive government, the few will be able to protect their inalienable interests.

So, I really don't see how liberals are guilty of either of the sins you cited. We believe that collective action is conducive to freedom in some instances, but certainly not in all. And liberal action, far from being an attempt to "play God," has been an effort to put into practice what most of the people believe will enhance their freedom to do as they choose.

• *American businessmen are witnessing the loss of their freedom due to interference by government bureaucrats.*

CONSERVATIVE: As a businessman, how can you tell me that individual freedom has actually increased over the past third of a century? Before the New Deal, men ran their businesses as they saw fit, not in accordance with the dictates of Washington professors and bureaucrats who had never made a sale or met a payroll. The basic decisions in a business—what and how much to produce, the amounts of capital and labor to be employed, and the means of financing and marketing output—were left to those who had invested their savings and assumed the risks. There was once a time when the market forces of supply and demand, not the president and union bosses, determined wages and prices. "Free enterprise" was more than a political slogan; it was the context in which American businesses operated and flourished. But liberals put an end to all of that.

Everywhere the businessman turns today he is confronted by the ubiquitous federal bureaucrat with his endless forms to fill out and rules to follow. Wages are arbitrarily pegged at a minimum of $1.25 an hour regardless of a firm's competitive position, costs, profit margin, and labor requirements. If the alternatives are unemployment at the minimum wage rate or employment at a slightly lower wage rate, the government insists on unemployment, no matter what the worker's preference might be. Washington fixes regulations governing working conditions, labor relations, stock issues, shipping rates, labeling, advertising, and nearly every other aspect of commerce. The only freedom business enjoys under liberal government is the freedom to comply with the bureaucracy's directives.

And, if you think businessmen suffer from undemocratic state supervision, take a look at the nation's farmers. In addition to the usual restrictions imposed by liberals, farmers are instructed what they can grow and how much they can sell. When the government claims the power to tell a man what he must do with his own land and labor, we are witnessing unblushing state socialism. Yes I know, all these agricultural controls are theoretically voluntary. But economic survival for those who refuse to conform is so difficult that few can afford to preserve their independence. The freedom to starve isn't worth much.

In short, "individual liberty" is an ironic watchword for a political philosophy which strips the productive persons in a society of their freedom of choice.

LIBERAL: Federal regulations of business and agriculture, like any other kind of government intervention, must be evaluated in terms of what is lost and what is gained. You limited yourself to reporting the losses.

I would never deny that controls over packaging and labeling prevent businessmen from managing their own property entirely as they please. But I must point out that these restrictions protect the consumer's freedom to make a rational choice between competing products. It would be ideal if the businessman's and the consumer's freedoms could both be maximized without regulating either. However, after many years of public complaint, Congress decided that government intervention was necessary to protect the interests of the consumer. Clearly, the regulation of the market place alone had not provided enough pressure to cause manufacturers to package and label their products honestly. To insure some equable balance between manufacturer and housewife, the government had to step in and provide some clear standards for manufacturers to meet. In other words, when all factors were considered and weighed, it was concluded that government intervention in this situation made available a more valued freedom than it eliminated.

Minimum-wage legislation is subject to a similar process of reasoning. Employers are explicitly denied the prerogative of paying their workers less than $1.25 an hour, which is not an arbitrary figure but a measure of mean subsistence. In return, unskilled, unorganized employees receive the freedom to earn a living wage, a freedom which many of them had previously lacked. Congress reasoned that, in a country as affluent as ours, the cost of enterprise includes the payment of wages that permit a decent standard of living. For a man working a forty-hour week, fifty-two weeks a year, $1.25 an hour comes to $2,600 annually—somewhat below the minimum nonpoverty income for family heads. Congress decided that sustaining those firms which could not meet this basic cost of human labor was far less important than insuring the working man's right to support himself and his family. Again the gain was thought to outweigh the loss.

In your discussion of farmers, your statement that the freedom to starve is worthless is indeed true. This is the best explanation of the government's desire to supervise certain agricultural matters. The prosperity of the "roaring twenties" never reached the American farmers. Increased farm production created by the unprecedented demands of World War I became surplus when European agriculture revived. Shrinking export opportunities and declining domestic prices cut the income of American farmers from 17.7 billion dollars in 1919 to 10.5 billion dollars in 1921. In desperation, individual farmers increased their output in the hope of avoiding bankruptcy. As you might expect, the result of this greater supply was to send prices spiraling lower and lower in the already glutted market.

The Crash on Wall Street made this difficult situation impossible. By 1932, farmer income was one-third of what it had been in the dismal agricultural year of 1929, and prices had fallen more than fifty percent. The first five years of the Depression saw three-quarters of a million farm families lose their homes and land through foreclosure and bankruptcy sales. At the time that FDR entered the White House, millions of farmers had been left with literally nothing but the freedom to starve.

It is in the light of these circumstances that the decision of President Roosevelt and Congress to enact various agricultural controls must be examined. They believed that the cost of inaction—the possible collapse of American agriculture—was far greater than the cost to the farmer of giving up his self-defeating freedom to grow as much as he wanted.

The federal government has insisted on local administration and a maximum of farmer participation in the carrying out of its program of agricultural controls. For example, no marketing quota can become effective without the approval of at least two-thirds of the growers of the commodity in question. If you think this is only a "rubber stamp" formality, talk to the officials of the Department of Agriculture who witnessed the rejection of their suggested wheat quota several years ago.

My point is simply that the recitation of freedoms *lost* when the government intervenes settles nothing. An exercise of federal power may be unwarranted and destructive, but this can't be determined without first having weighed expected losses against expected gains and the price of nonintervention.

As for the last thirty years, I think the country has come out way ahead. The principle of "consumer as sovereign" has been strengthened by numerous government safeguards while, at the same time, as statistics demonstrate, the businessman has retained the basic freedom to earn a reasonable return on his investments and energy. Certain specific freedoms may have been destroyed in the process, but almost always they have been exchanged for alternatives shown to be more satisfactory in the long run.

• *Wasteful government spending and the confiscatory income tax hobble individual liberty.*

CONSERVATIVE: No discussion of liberty in America can be concluded without some reference to taxes. Taxation is yet another way in which liberals reduce individual freedom. Whenever I mention this to liberal acquaintances, they always respond: "Taxes are merely a problem of public finance." But they have missed the central issue.

A fundamental tenet of natural law is man's right to the possession of and use of his property, and that includes his income as well as his house and car. Without the material means to do what he wants, the individual cannot be free. By confiscating a portion of each man's income in the form of taxes, the government destroys his freedom.

LIBERAL: Where did you get this notion of "confiscation"?

CONSERVATIVE: Let me finish. As Barry Goldwater wrote "How can a man be free if the fruits of his labor are not his to dispose of, but are treated instead as part of a common pool of public wealth? Property and freedom are inseparable; to the extent government takes the one in the form of taxes, it intrudes on the other." I hasten to add that, on the average, about thirty-three percent of every dollar we currently earn is siphoned off by taxes of one sort or another.

We find ourselves in this tragic state because liberals have somehow convinced the public that the government has an unlimited claim on our earnings. Now, I believe that every citizen has an obligation to support the legitimate functions of government, but only those functions which are legitimate. Taxation to finance activities not delegated to the federal government by the Constitution falls outside Washington's rightful claim on our incomes. Yet most of our tax money presently goes for unconstitutional, liberal welfare schemes.

Individual freedom will continue to die in this country until the American people have the good sense to elect a conservative government committed to cutting taxes and spending to their proper sizes.

LIBERAL: I don't think the state necessarily has any claim on our incomes. If the American people decided that they wanted a national government only so that they could attend a presidential inaugural ball quadrennially, the revenue needed to sustain such a government could be raised by selling federal Bingo licenses, and most of us would never have to send a penny to Washington. Our taxes are not simply determined by some abstract formula, but by the specific services that we request from our government.

You quoted Barry Goldwater as saying "Property and freedom are inseparable; to the extent government takes the one in the form of taxes, it intrudes on the other." If we still agree that freedom is the absence of restraint to do what you want, it strikes me that the judicious use of taxation increases the individual's freedom rather than intruding on it.

We are all limited to one degree or another by the size of our income; a dollar will only buy so much. Were there any way to make this dollar go farther, we would have more available alternatives and, hence, more freedom. And this is precisely what wise taxation does. The average American would have to save all his earnings for 500 years to purchase one jet plane to protect his house from possible enemies, and by the time he had finished paying for it, the plane would be obsolete and his reflexes would be too slow for him to fly it. However, by contributing to the federal government about $400 a year (the defense allotment from the taxes of the head of a family earning $5,600 a year) this same American is afforded the strongest military defense in the world, including thousands of jet aircraft.

No one likes to breathe noxious, foul air. If people had to deal with this health hazard privately, it would cost every family a fortune. Special filtering systems would have to be purchased along with heaven knows how much Airwick. By spending tax money to clean up our air, the job can be done more effectively at a trivial expense to each citizen. In other words, the tax dollar can often buy a lot more for the individual than that same dollar in personal income would buy.

CONSERVATIVE: Applying this same argument, how do you justify taxes to support giveaway programs like the War on Poverty? After all, not many people initiate such efforts on their own, so it doesn't make sense to talk about "stretching dollars that would be spent anyway."

LIBERAL: I can't agree with you. Society has committed itself to keeping the poor alive. This requires several billion dollars in state and local taxes every year. The objective of the War on Poverty is to invest a little more money initially in those who are potentially productive in the hope of getting them off the relief roles and saving a lot of money in the long run. I say "invest," not "spend," because returns of a very real sort are expected. It is more profitable from both a social and economic point of view to help a poor person become self-reliant than to keep him, his children, and his children's children feeding out of the public hand for the rest of their lives. It makes sense in hard cash terms, even if the humanitarian aspects of the program do not interest you.

As to which functions of government are proper and deserving of tax support and which are not, we've already debated that. Besides, in considering total federal expenditures and tax collections, it doesn't make as much difference as you might think whose definition of "legitimate" we adopt.

Let's take a look at the federal government's budget for the fiscal year 1966 (June 30, 1965, through July 1, 1966). During this period the government plans to spend slightly less than 100 billion dollars. Of this amount, 51.5 billion dollars is earmarked for national defense. Adding the 4.6 billion dollars for veterans' benefits and services, and the 11.6 billion dollars in interest payments on the national debt (two-thirds of which was incurred fighting World War II) we have already accounted for 67.7 billion dollars, or two-thirds of the entire administrative budget.

CONSERVATIVE: But 33 billion dollars is not exactly a negligible sum. What about the remaining expenditures?

LIBERAL: Roughly 4 billion dollars is allocated for international affairs. Of this, the largest single chunk is the 1.7 billion dollars for the Food for Peace program, which uses our agricultural surplus to help feed hungry people around the world. 870 million dollars goes for long-term loans to help underdeveloped countries get their economies moving. 390 million dollars buys equipment and technical training for countries like Vietnam, whose political and economic stability is vital to our own security, and 390 million dollars is being invested in our Alliance for Progress program in Latin America. Space research and exploration take another 5.1 billion dollars—sixty-two percent of which is being spent to put an American on the moon. 2.69 billion dollars is used for conservation and developing the nation's natural resources. Two-thirds of this total goes to finance flood-control and irrigation projects, improved navigation, the building and maintenance of power plants in areas where private installations aren't profitable, and the management of 464 million acres of public lands in the Western states and in Alaska. The administration of national forests and parks consumes the rest. 2.8 billion dollars is authorized for commerce and transportation, which includes the highway program (sixty percent of the commerce and transportation outlay), the Post Office (which will cost about 700 million dollars to run in 1966), and aviation and water transport investments.

Adding these expenses to the 67.7 billion dollars spent for defense, veterans, and debt interest brings the total accounted for to 82.3 billion dollars—more than four-fifths of the budget. I seriously doubt that conservatives would find much to cut from this list.

As for the final 17.4 billion dollars, about half (8.33 billion dollars) is used for health, labor, and welfare services. This includes 3.5 billion dollars for public assistance programs administered by state and local governmental units for the blind, the disabled, the aged, and dependent young people who are being raised by mothers with insufficient income. It also includes 2.2 billion dollars for health services and research in mental and physical health; 1.35 billion dollars for the War on Poverty, designed to make self-sufficient citizens out of nonproductive persons; 1.1 billion dollars to retrain workers with obsolete skills or no skills; 402 million dollars for school lunch and special milk programs for children whose parents must send them to school hungry; and 326 million dollars for vocational rehabilitation. These are what conservatives are fond of calling the "liberal giveaway programs."

Of the 9.0 billion dollars left, about forty-five percent (3.94 billion dollars) is authorized for agriculture—2.7 billion dollars

for farm income stabilization, and the rest for loans and research. Education is receiving 2.6 billion dollars, primarily for
aid to state and local schools. The last item in the budget is for
government operations: 2.46 billion dollars. Since this is an expense that occasions much controversy, let me break it down for
you. It costs 853 million dollars to collect federal taxes, 596 million dollars for property and records management, 388 million
dollars for protective services and alien control (the bulk of this
goes to the Federal Bureau of Investigation), 243 million dollars
for legislative and judicial functions, 213 million dollars for services and assistance to U.S. territories, possessions, and depend-
encies (the Virgin Islands, Ryukyu Islands, American Samoa,
the Trust Territory of the Pacific, and Guam), and 169 million
dollars for central personnel management, such as the administrative costs of the Civil Service Commission.

This is the federal budget. I don't doubt that a conservative
president and Congress would eliminate some spending that liberals consider important, but this talk about cutting government
expenditures in half is a lot of nonsense. If conservatives were to
try to cut federal outlays by ten percent—and I doubt that this
would be possible—the 10 billion dollars "saved" would figure
out to about $50 per person. This would not expand anyone's
opportunity to do what he wants by any meaningful amount.
And it seems to me most likely that the programs and services
sacrificed would result in a net loss of freedom for Americans.

2
Human nature
and the welfare state

Thomas Hobbes, the seventeenth-century English philosopher, characterized the existence of man as being "nasty, brutish and short." We can see a somewhat similar viewpoint about man in the minds of present-day conservatives. They seem to see man as being naturally slothful, lazy, and wasteful, a condition which fails to account for the ruin of us all only because man's natural fear of privation drives him on to compete in the human arena for food and the other necessities of life. As Hobbes so aptly put it, the natural state of man "is the war of each against all," and the conservatives, seeking as little modification of this natural state as possible, square off against the liberal welfare state as being a corrupter of human nature and a destroyer of human incentive.

Their argument is quite simple. Since man is lazy, when you give him what he needs to live, he will lose interest in work, become shiftless, and regress to his naturally indolent ways.

The conservatives consider this concept of man to be so basic as to be self-evident, so they offer little in substantiation of it. However, as one of the keystones to their whole idea of the rela-

tion of the state to man, this concept must be dealt with care-
fully. As in formal logic, if you accept the initial assumption,
you must be prepared to accept the proof that follows.

More on this later.

Another point made by various conservative spokesmen is
that the mass society and bureaucracy engendered by liberal
government swallows the individual, destroys his individuality,
and makes him into an automaton—all in the name of progress.
Again, while we find no empirical description of how this is
done, this is thought by the conservative to be a self-evident,
rather easily revealed result of liberal machinations. "Just look
around you," conservatives say. "Isn't everyone much more in-
terested in conforming than in striking out on his own?"

Thus, conservatives see welfare liberalism not as a program
of uplift, but merely as a device of leveling everyone down to the
lowest common denominator.

These ideas form the basis for discussion in this chapter. But,
instead of attempting to formulate our discussion in these broad,
vague terms, let us instead discuss the questions of character,
individuality, and conformism in terms of specific political pro-
grams.

• *Those liberal cradle-to-the-grave security schemes weaken*
character and stifle individual initiative.

CONSERVATIVE: Your claim that the welfare state or, as you
prefer to call it, "positive" government is the means to a freer
and more productive society contains one serious contradiction
that destroys your entire case. By supplying people with security from the cradle to the grave, you kill their initiative. They
lose their desire to achieve and accomplish anything. It is human
nature: if I can get something for nothing, why should I knock
myself out working for it?

Think about the consequences of what you are advocating. If

you gave your child his allowance every week whether he took out the garbage or not, your house would be impossible to live in within ten days!

Seriously, people need personal incentive, even the fear of starvation, in order to be productive. Assure them that they will be able to live comfortably without doing their share of the work, and they will become passive and apathetic—useless.

Liberalism's pledge to abolish fear of want by means of the welfare state is very high sounding and humanitarian, but it can't work. Able-bodied adults must be confronted continually with the threat that if they do not work, they will not eat. You may accuse me of holding a cynical view of man and his nature, but experience shows it to be correct. By creating a welfare system in which the state will care for everyone no matter what, you are ignoring human nature and hastening the day when we will be a nation of self-satisfied, nonproductive vegetables. To borrow Pope's description, American man will be:

> Fixed like a plant on his peculiar spot,
> To draw nutrition, propagate, and rot.

One irony of the welfare state is that it actually harms the people it is designed to help. Poverty is more a set of attitudes than a material condition. Notice how quickly the modern housing developments we've built for the city's low-income families become slums again.

The liberal social planners in Washington seem to be unable to comprehend the human organism. If you put a man on the dole or create some sort of trumped-up form of "make work" to keep him busy when he's down and out, you do a great deal of damage to his character. Instead of encouraging hard work and determination in an individual, a welfare check can only reinforce the state of mind that led to his impoverishment.

By giving him a handout, you have told the welfare recipient in effect, "Keep your lazy, shiftless, unambitious ways and you will be rewarded"—at least with ample welfare checks every month.

You simply reinforce a vicious circle. Give a woman with two illegitimate children a regular check from Aid to Dependent Children funds, tell her that she'll get more if she has more children, and she will be tempted to have more illegitimate children. If you don't think this is what actually happens, check with the city welfare department.

Call me hard-hearted if you like, but I would rather see a few poor people in this country than an entire nation of complacent nonproducers.

I am not advocating that we should neglect those who are too old, too young, or too ill to earn their own living. But why not take care of them privately? With private charity, everyone understands that the donation is not an obligation, but a product of the giver's generosity. As Goldwater explained, when you reduce charity to a mechanical operation of government, you blunt man's nobler impulses.

Any way you look at it, the welfare state defeats its avowed ends by destroying individual initiative and encouraging idleness. Your claims that liberal programs serve to develop individual aspiration and character are simply unfounded.

LIBERAL: The soundness of your charge depends on certain basic assumptions. You have assumed, first, that man by nature is a passive, inert animal who will arouse himself to effort only when prodded by the threat of deprivation; second, that assistance will only corrode what will power man does possess; and, third, that any effort to tamper with this simple input-output mechanism will only serve to warp the fabric of our society. I do not believe that either our common experience or contemporary social science will support these assumptions.

If your assumptions were true, we would have to conclude that the lowest economic groups—those people who are existing right at the level of subsistence—are the most active and productive individuals in our society. But surveys show that the poor belong to the fewest number of social groups, are the least active in public affairs, finish the fewest years of school, and make the smallest economic contribution to the nation. In other words, those people who are closest to the struggle for survival and who, according to your assumptions, ought to have the most incentive to be active, are the most inactive and least productive members of the community.

Look at it the other way around. Those two gentlemen whom conservatives defer to so often, Barry Goldwater and William Buckley, were not born with hunger staring them in the face, yet they are energetic and productive persons. The same holds for the Kennedys, the Rockefellers, the Fords, and several million other wealthy Americans. Although they were all born into families with so-called "womb to tomb" security surpassing anything a government could provide, most of them are useful citizens. According to your theory, these fortunate individuals should be contentedly languishing in their penthouses doing absolutely nothing. But this isn't the case.

Men labor for many things: security, power, prestige, the joy of workmanship. Few of us work just for food and shelter. Once people are sure of the material essentials of life, they normally find other, usually more creative outlets for their physical and intellectual energies.

But let's not be satisfied with our own observations. The social sciences, notably psychology and anthropology, are in general agreement that man is an innately active creature. For example, recent anthropological studies have discovered that the natives of certain islands of the South Pacific, long described by armchair authorities as living in blissful indolence, work and work hard despite the fact that they, almost uniquely in the world, are furnished by nature with all the material necessities. In a set of experiments involving the more "civilized" peoples of the West, subjects were paid $20 an hour to lie motionless in a dark room. Most couldn't take it for more than a few hours; their body chemistry was such that they had to be doing things.

Now let's examine the effects of the welfare programs you

have called into question. For example, let's look at social insurance, far and away the largest welfare program. By means of the various programs within our social-security system—old-age insurance, disability insurance, medical insurance for the aged—the risk of those expenses which often beset people through no fault of their own is spread over the entire population. This coverage against accidents, such as injuries on the job, and inevitabilities, such as old age and retirement, is not government charity. The benefits are paid out of a trust fund to which all participants contribute during their working years. You don't hear people accuse commercial insurance policies of destroying individual initiative and character. Since public insurance operates on the same principles, there is no basis for such accusations here either.

CONSERVATIVE: But you are overlooking a crucial difference. Commercial insurance is voluntary, but social security is compulsory.

LIBERAL: This distinction is important when we're talking about premiums; it has little or no effect on individual incentive. In the first place, with both private and public insurance, you have to contribute funds in order to receive benefits. In neither case does anyone "get something for nothing."

And, as a more general point, I know of no evidence that compulsion weakens character. In our state, for example, it's mandatory that every driver carry accident insurance. Does the knowledge that the costs of an accident will be covered by this insurance stifle the driver's incentive to earn a living? Or take a look at banks. Banks have to belong to the Federal Deposit Insurance Corporation, which insures all individual savings accounts for losses up to $10,000, but I have never heard a banker say that this undermines his incentive to keep his bank solvent.

Therefore, compulsory public insurance is no more a help or a hindrance to the development of individual character than private insurance. If you agree that the latter is harmless in this respect, I think you'll have to conclude that the former also is.

To sum up, the purpose of national social insurance is to distribute risks widely enough to afford all citizens, except the long-term unemployed, minimal protection against severe deprivation. This has the effect of setting a material limit—a none too attractive one at that—below which society will not permit the individual to fall.

A second type of welfare program provides temporary subsistence incomes for those who are able-bodied but unemployed for a reason society deems acceptable. The most obvious examples are unemployment insurance, which is primarily a state program, and Aid to Dependent Children. In our complex industrial economy, huge forces like technology and the business cycle often result in unemployment. While the individual worker is laid off for reasons such as these, which are clearly beyond his control, he is supplied with enough income to sustain himself and his family. If, however, he was fired because of poor workmanship, continued absence, or some other personal inadequacy, he does not qualify for unemployment benefits. These subsistence payments are not a dole, but the benefits being paid on a social-insurance policy to which the worker has contributed during times of employment. The payments are limited by law in duration and amount, which prevents anyone from living off them indefinitely.

In establishing the Aid to Dependent Children program, Congress made the judgment that it is a wise social investment to enable a woman to remain home and raise her fatherless children. This aid is temporary also, terminating when the children grow up.

CONSERVATIVE: But we both know people who abuse these programs.

LIBERAL: Sure we do. There will always be dishonest souls who will use the welfare system to cheat the government and the taxpayers. But, as long as they remain a fractional minority they present no excuse for belittling the great value of the welfare programs. According to a recent study, only about 1.2 percent and 5.4 percent respectively do misrepresent the facts in applying for benefits from these two programs.

This brings us to the third type of welfare program, those designed to help the poor. According to the criteria set up by the people conducting the War on Poverty, to be considered poor you must have less than sixty-nine cents a day for all your food (twenty-three cents a meal) and less than $1.40 a day to cover all other expenses, such as rent, clothing, transportation, and recreation. Using this measure of poverty, thirty-five million Americans, fifteen million of them children, are poor today. If these criteria are raised slightly to ninety cents a day for food and $1.60 a day for all other expenses, fifty-two million Americans—more than one out of every four persons living in this country—would qualify as poverty-stricken.

In studying the causes of poverty, I quite agree with you that attitudes play an important part. Being poor is a mental as well as physical state of being. However, I really don't see though how the mental state of either the very young or the very old helps contribute to their condition, and these people constitute over half of America's poor. You're right in pointing to the poor as essentially different from the rest of us. Michael Harrington, a noted writer on the subject of poverty, argues that the poor feel shut out from the middle class and that they lack the aspiration to better themselves because they feel alienated in "the other America." Attitudes must be changed, but when you say that the poor are such because they lack the desire to get out of their poverty or because they are lazy, you simply state the problem and do not solve it.

CONSERVATIVE: But you've missed my point that to support the poor on welfare encourages their laziness and destroys any reasons they might have had for wanting to change.

LIBERAL: I am getting to that. Let's put these welfare programs into some sort of perspective. As I said before, there are no federal welfare payments to the potentially employable poor except Aid to Dependent Children, which is a special case. So I will use unemployment insurance, which is a state program, as my example. In 1964, six million workers—less than eight percent of the labor force—received unemployment benefits. These benefits averaged $36 a week for an average of thirteen weeks. Too many people seem to think that being on welfare is the key to a ranch house in suburbia and the easy life in general. In fact, existing on welfare allows subsistence on the meanest level and no more. If $36 a week were the only thing out of life most men craved, I imagine we would quit our jobs today and live off the government. However, I think I can speak for both of us in concluding that this is not a very attractive prospect.

At a cost of eleven billion dollars a year—less than 1.7 percent of our gross national product—the government could eliminate poverty by distributing money to all the poor. But this is not what the government is doing. Liberals have long agreed with you that neither the make-work programs nor the dole is a cure for poverty. This is why the new War on Poverty and related programs are designed to provide the impoverished with the encouragement and the means to escape their condition. Instead of handouts, the poor are receiving wages for their work while they receive training in the skills that they need to be employable. The goal of these projects is to transform welfare recipients into taxpayers who can contribute to the wealth of the nation instead of being a drain upon it.

But traditional techniques for reducing poverty will no longer work. Today's poor bear little resemblance to their pre-World War I counterparts. The millions of immigrants who streamed through Ellis Island into the slums of the great industrial cities at the turn of the century were, as a rule, desperately poor. However, their presence in this new world, with their alien tongues and unfamiliar customs, was proof of their determination to build a better life; and, more often than not, their drive and desire enabled their sons and daughters to make the jump into the middle class.

The poverty-stricken of 1965, however, know little of the American dream. They are the disillusioned product of lost hope and forgotten aspiration. This hard core of second-generation and third-generation poor were somehow left behind by the rest of the country, and many of them have resigned themselves to never catching up. Job opportunities for such dispirited persons are not enough, nor is training and education. Our new antipoverty programs attempt to provide proper education and training, with efforts to create a will to compete and assimilate. Without this change of attitude, the poor will be locked in their poverty and will raise children even further beyond our reach.

Of course we cannot be sure that these new programs will achieve all their ends; but it is obvious that ignoring the plight of the poor will only lead to longer relief rolls for our children's generation to support, and the legacy of a weaker America.

I am glad that we agree that those who are too young, too elderly, or too infirm to support themselves should not be left in the streets to starve. But what happens when we leave their care to private charities?

As you explained, it is important to preserve a man's dignity and pride. Obviously, being too young, too old, or too sick to earn your keep is hardly grounds for blame or punishment. Yet, without government social-welfare programs, the elderly or incapacitated person has just two choices: he can go hat in hand to a private charity or he can sit and wait for someone to guess that he needs help. The first choice leaves him neither pride nor dignity; the second may leave him his pride—at the expense of nutrition, decent surroundings, and relief from daily uncertainty and frequent desperation.

The social-security system gives him both pride and dignity through a third choice: He can reap the benefits of an insurance policy to which he contributed when he was working. If he is one of those who never worked enough to qualify for social security because of poor mental or physical health, American standards of decency require that his basic needs be met in an orderly fashion, not through the haphazard programs inherent in the nature of private charity. This is not to say that private charity has no place. On the contrary, its contributions fill important gaps between the efforts of officialdom and those of the individual. But liberals believe that our government, as an instrument of the collective will, has the residual responsibility for the subsistence of every individual. We believe this very policy is what makes possible the pride and dignity we all want for the aged, the ill, and the young of our society.

I think you will have to agree that the purpose of our limited welfare state is not to breed apathy and idleness, but to free people to be more creative and productive. To a degree, we have succeeded in attaining these aims. If not every program has been a total success, this does not prove that the principles underlying the welfare state are unsound, but simply that we still have a lot to learn.

• *The "progressive" income tax kills individual and corporate initiative by punishing those who have the get-up-and-go to get something done.*

CONSERVATIVE: It is not only what you give a man that can stifle his initiative and weaken his incentive, it can also be what you take from him. A good example of this type of destruction of initiative is the confiscatory "progressive" income tax which the federal government collects. You may argue that giving a man something for nothing does not rob him of his incentive to work, but you must admit that seizing the fruits of his labor will discourage maximum effort on his part.

With welfare programs you reward shiftlessness; with the "progressive" income tax you punish success. One makes as little sense as the other.

Many businessmen today say they refuse to expand their businesses or buy new ones because the increased profits would put them in a higher tax bracket and make the extra work of running the new enterprise hardly worth their while. Just think about this "progressive" income tax which claims anywhere from fourteen to sixty-five percent of a man's income—can you imagine working as much as thirty-four weeks out of the year just so the government can redistribute your earnings to people who aren't as capable or hard-working as you are? This tax obviously discourages our best people from building their businesses and finding new and more efficient ways of doing things. We need a tax structure which generates economic growth and development by claiming an equal percentage of each man's income and no more, not a method of taxation which holds us back; and this applies equally to individuals and corporations. Instead of giving us a real progressive income tax, Washington has actually saddled us with a regressive tax.

LIBERAL: I admit that the first time I paid my income tax I reached the same conclusion as you: The tax system is bad! Later, at a more rational moment, I realized that tax theory has no firm answers. It can be argued convincingly that a tax schedule which hits the highest income groups with the highest rate of tax impedes commerce and stunts the growth of big business. It can be argued equally well that a progressive tax rate plus the desire for a high standard of living induces people to work harder than ever. If an entrepreneur wants to live in a certain manner and the government takes a proportionately larger part of his income as he moves up the scale, he will be motivated to increase his earnings to afford the luxuries he wants. This usually entails longer hours, greater effort, expanding capital, and increased efficiency on his part—all necessary conditions if the economy is to grow.

Unfortunately, the economists have not resolved this dilemma. They report that there is little conclusive evidence to support either case.

So we must turn from theory to performance. A glance at the national economy during the years of the Kennedy-Johnson administration forcefully deflates the notion that individual and corporate income cannot grow—and grow spectacularly—while a progressive tax schedule is operative. Between 1961 and 1965, disposable personal income (that is, the money available for individual expenditure after taxes) increased twenty-four percent, from $350 billion to $432 billion; at the same time, corporate profits after taxes recorded a spectacular jump of forty-four percent, from 22 billion dollars to 31.6 billion dollars.

There may be, of course, some point at which the tax schedule becomes too progressive, so that individual and corporate incentives to earn and produce are discouraged. In revising the limits of the tax schedule recently from twenty to ninety-one percent to fourteen to sixty-five percent, Congress acknowledged this possibility and took steps to forestall it. But there is no evidence that the economy is impeded by taxes today. Business is booming, and the consumer is buying goods and services as never before.

• *Liberalism promotes conformity at the expense of individuality, forcing every one to the lowest common denominator.*

CONSERVATIVE: Why do liberals insist on working toward an egalitarian society in which individualism is abandoned for conformity and the government labors to force us all down to the same mediocre level? Going against human nature is both foolhardy and dangerous.

I am the first to maintain that all men are equal in the eyes of God and should enjoy equal opportunity and equal justice under the law. But that is a far cry from saying that all men possess the same abilities, aspirations, and needs. This, I believe, is one of the key differences between conservative and liberal thinking. Conservatives insist on viewing men as unique individuals, while liberals frame their thoughts in terms of the "common man" or the "collective will." Only a philosophy which recognizes the essential differences between men and seeks to develop their varying potentials can claim to be in harmony with nature.

As usual, the welfare state can be found operating in the opposite direction. The progressive income tax and the myriad of giveaway programs it subsidizes combine to enforce a false economic equality on the populace by taking from the rich and giving to the poor without due reason.

What happened to the grand dreams and plans the young people of past generations used to harbor? Today's young people settle for identical-looking houses in identical-looking suburbs and membership in identical country clubs, all leading to identical retirement plans, and all paid for by identical corporate or government bureaucratic jobs. Some American dream!

You can rave about the virtues of the "common man" and his "average" existence. But history is wrought by very uncommon characters. If liberals persist in fostering these unnatural ideas of egalitarianism and conformity, the United States is going to find itself sorely wanting in those extraordinary individuals who lead nations and make them great.

LIBERAL: There you go again, trying to trap me with that old "when will you stop beating your wife" argument. Liberals have never regarded all men as essentially similar, nor have they tried to make them so. Personally, I like John Adams' contention that we are not seeking egalitarianism in America but rather the opportunity for every man to be unequal.

Let's go back to the Great Depression, when the desperate economic situation gave a liberal president and Congress a relatively free hand to implement the programs they wanted. One of their first creations was the Works Progress Administration (WPA) under Harry Hopkins, which initiated a series of projects offering individuals jobs in the areas of their interest and ability. Playwrights were put to work providing original material for the WPA federal theater project which traveled the country bringing the excitement of live theater to those who had never known it. Bricklayers were hired to build schools, libraries, and hospitals. The results of their efforts, playwrights and bricklayers alike, is a monument to the New Deal's recognition that individuals *do* possess differing abilities and aspirations. After all, it would have been much simpler to put everyone to work raking leaves.

Since then, government programs have been established to combat poverty, to provide vocational and other specialized training, and to treat emotional and physical disorders. These programs are based on the premise that individuals confront life and its challenges in varying environments, equipped with dissimilar intellectual and psychological tools. The War on Poverty is not designed to make all men the same. On the contrary, it works to increase opportunity, to give each individual the greatest possible chance to develop his potential as he pleases. This should not be confused with forcing everyone to use his opportunities in a similar fashion—a stifling practice which liberals have never advocated. Instead, recognize that equalized opportunity means more freedom for more individuals to pursue their own versions of the American dream.

There is no contesting your statement that welfare programs and progressive taxes serve to redistribute some income from the wealthier to the poorer. But has the purpose been to drive all Americans to the same standard of living? No. The goal has been to provide the education and training and create the economic conditions which will enable the poor to escape their poverty. We know that the paradox of appalling want amidst great plenty is no longer necessary in our affluent society.

What have been the results of this effort? Though it may sound contradictory, there has been a lot of lifting up but not much leveling down. Whereas two-thirds of America was "ill-clothed and ill-fed" in 1933, this fearsome fraction has been reduced to one-fifth today. At the same time the upper economic groups, who bear the brunt of progressive taxation, have been relatively unaffected.

How is this possible? It is true that if the U.S. economy has remained stagnant since 1933, every extra dollar earned by American working men would have to have been at the expense of more affluent members of society. But—and this is my key point—the U.S. economy has not remained the same size over the past third of a century. It has expanded enormously in *real* money terms. The government has helped promote this expansion by using tax revenue to stimulate growth and to prepare and educate the indigent so that they could contribute to that growth and share in its fruits. Most of the additional income of the former poor has come from that tremendous economic expansion, not from welfare handouts of money taxed from the middle and upper classes. And the multiplier effect of the expansion has made this uplift possible with little leveling of incomes in the top brackets.

Let's examine your charge that liberal government is causing attitudes of conformity, especially among younger people. If conformity is on the upswing, I suggest that it is up to you to demonstrate that the liberal philosophy and its programs are the cause of this conformity. Is there proof, or even an indication, of a causal link between the two? Let's not find ourselves in the ludicrous position of blaming a liberal government for everything that has happened in this country since March 4, 1933— including such phenomena as the near extinction of the white egret.

What I've been trying to show is that liberals abhor the idea of a faceless egalitarian society fully as much as conservatives do, and that the liberal welfare state has consistently respected and encouraged individuality. What is more, liberals believe in positive action to *promote* individual opportunity by encouraging people to unite in searching for the solution to common problems.

• *Liberals see only the economic side of man and not his spiritual side. They fail to take the whole man into account.*

CONSERVATIVE: We both claim that our chief concern is the individual, but we are not speaking of the same individual. The dangerous distortion in the liberals' perception of the individual —the distortion which Barry Goldwater rightly regards as "the root difference between the Conservatives and the Liberals of today"—is their failure to see beyond the economic side of man. Liberals take into account only the material aspect of man's nature, while conservatives recognize that man is both an economic animal and a spiritual creature. Because conservatives believe that man has spiritual needs and spiritual desires which take precedence over his economic wants, they think and act with a view to the "whole" man.

If I may quote Barry Goldwater again, because he addresses himself to this question so effectively: "Conservatism therefore looks upon the enhancement of man's spiritual nature as the primary concern of political philosophy. Liberals, on the other hand, regard the satisfaction of economic wants as the dominant mission of society."

The best proof that we really do view the individual differently can be found by looking back at the terms in which we've couched our arguments so far. You have talked unceasingly about economic opportunity, social insurance, the growth of corporate profits—about money in every shape and form. Meanwhile, I've been trying to get you to take a look at man's freedom, at his character, at the factors that cause him to show initiative, at the elements that constitute his spiritual being.

As long as you continue to deny the spiritual side of man, you can hardly claim that the objective of the liberal welfare state is the development of the whole individual.

LIBERAL: Before you decide whether we see half a man, two-thirds of a man, or the whole man, may I suggest that we look behind those economic figures and programs I've been discussing.

Whenever I have mentioned the goal of welfare programs, it has been in terms of freeing the noneconomic aspects of man, his hopes, aspirations, abilities, and intellect from the economic bonds of poverty and the fear of want. What man can devote his time and thoughts to education, religion, civic affairs, the arts, or even to decent family life, when he is forced to fight every waking minute for the substance and security to sustain his family?

What about those men, women, and children who worked in the factories and mines in the early days of the industrial revolution in Britain for eighty or one hundred hours a week at subsistence wages? Were they able to develop their spiritual life? History recreates them for us as a race of sooty, stunted people whose only respite from their eternal labor was an occasional mug of ale or a cock fight.

Liberals have never advocated economic advance and a monetary social security as the ultimate ends of society. Rather, they regard them as the quantitative means which can liberate a man to develop himself qualitatively—spiritually and intellectually—in whatever manner he pleases. That is the aim of "the Great Society." Eighty percent of the American people have escaped from conditions of actual poverty; they live in some comfort, reasonably secure in the knowledge that they will never have to depend on charity or spend the closing days of their lives in a county poorhouse. But, as President Johnson has repeatedly declared, this is not the end; it is just the beginning of a new phase in which the individual will have the leisure to develop the spiritual side of his nature and in which national development will increasingly pursue noneconomic goals: better education, improved health, wider participation in the arts, and the beautification of our cities and countryside.

Perhaps it is the conservatives who should take another look at their concept of the individual. With their theory that man will be robbed of all incentive and initiative, weakened in character, and doomed to mediocrity if the fear of material want is removed from his life, it appears to be the conservatives who view man as fundamentally material in motivation.

Man is both spiritual and economic. But to declare his spiritual freedom and fail to sunder his economic shackles is the height of futility; the accomplishment of both is essential to the individual's fulfillment.

• *The result of three decades of the welfare state has been national moral decay.*

CONSERVATIVE: You keep urging me to forget theory and common sense and to rely on past performance and actual effects in evaluating the liberal welfare state. All right, let's see what a third of a century of liberal national government has done to the American character.

There used to be a time when a person could walk any street in this town late at night with absolutely no fear for his safety. Today you would not permit your wife or daughter out alone in most parts of the city after dark, and you yourself have to think twice about entering certain areas with no means of protection. What has happened? Under liberal government the crime rate has shot up spectacularly, especially among juveniles, to the point where we are even afraid to leave our houses at night.

These are not the only signs of our moral decay. The divorce rate has doubled since the 1920's. Alcoholism and narcotics addiction have risen steadily until they have become commonplace. The proportion of unwed mothers is far greater today than it was thirty years ago, with the largest increase among teen-age girls. Our newsstands and book stores are filled with pornography. The movies and television are preoccupied with sex and violence.

My fifteen-year-old daughter had a party last weekend in our basement. The dances they did looked like aboriginal pre-mating rites; even I was embarrassed.

Values which used to be taught at home or by the church, such as honesty, diligence, and parental respect, are laughed at as "old fashioned" by the younger generation. The moral fiber of this nation has so deteriorated that "do it if you can get away with it" is fast replacing the Golden Rule. This is what liberal government has to show for three decades in Washington; this is the record upon which it is basing its claim to the future.

LIBERAL: I did indeed suggest that you judge liberalism by what it has done for better or worse; but this implies limiting your critical examples to things on which liberal principles or practices have had some effect. Your description of contemporary America may be accurate, but you must demonstrate some causal links between liberal government and this moral decay you say we are experiencing. What is the connection? What do you think liberal government has done to promote increased crime and divorce? Just how has the welfare state been responsible for weakening the nation's moral fiber?

CONSERVATIVE: In the first place, liberal government itself hasn't exactly been a model of ethical conduct for the country to follow, with the Bobby Baker scandal and similar sordid affairs. Furthermore, as I stated earlier, liberal welfare programs tend to weaken individual responsibility and family ties, two factors that used to act as a check against crime and other immoral behavior. But my main criticism is not what liberals have done to undermine values, but that they have done virtually nothing to reestablish the values we have lost. The situation has been steadily deteriorating, and liberals have been sitting back as if the problem did not exist.

LIBERAL: Now our discussion has substance. Yes, the liberals have the Bobby Baker fiasco to be ashamed of. However, the conservatives had the Teapot Dome scandals of the 1920's, which involved even larger sums of money. Corruption finds its way into all governments and is no respecter of political philosophy. Constant vigilance by large numbers of citizens, liberal and conservative alike, is the price of honesty in government.

We have already considered at some length your charge that welfare programs weaken character. We both agree that most men think of their responsibility to themselves and to their families as more than just the providing of material subsistence. How can you say that social-insurance plans destroy this responsibility? Liberals think it is the other way around: the security these programs offer and the increased opportunities they bring help many individuals to fulfill their responsibilities, not to abandon them. Aid to Dependent Children, for instance, performs very effectively its function of helping families to stay together.

You say that liberal government does nothing to stem the moral breakdown which you see taking place across the nation. Let's examine your evidence.

Crime has been on the upswing in recent years, though much of the increase in juvenile delinquency is due to the increasing proportion of young people in the population. What are the reasons for this rising crime rate? No one knows for certain. Some juvenile crime is committed by young people from affluent families who have failed to acquire nonmaterial interests at home and in school, and do it for "kicks." But by far the greatest number of crimes is still accounted for by the slum dwellers of our big cities. The rising expectations of the poor make some of them impatient—especially the young ones. Eliminating poverty can go a long way toward reducing this antisocial activity.

I am still not clear what you think the government should do. In so far as poverty and inadequate education generate crime and the abandonment of moral values, liberals in government have been working since the first days of the New Deal to eliminate the former and improve the latter. If you are saying that we ought to press these campaigns more vigorously, I would agree; but this would put you in the strange position of claiming that liberal government is doing too much while demanding that it do more. Beyond this, I do not see what else the government can or should do. In a democracy, morality is a matter of individual judgment so long as it doesn't harm other members of the society. You will have to supply me with some more concrete suggestions.

• *Today Americans are a pampered, overfed lot. The rugged individual is a man of the past.*

CONSERVATIVE: I would like to end this discussion of the liberal welfare state's effect on individual character and initiative with an observation which sounds a little vague, but which describes a very real condition. Over the past three decades, Americans have become "soft." I know you want names, facts, and dates to document this contention, but physical and spiritual deterioration aren't best understood as statistics. All you have to do is look at what is going on around you to become aware of the "flabbiness" which has beset most Americans.

It can be viewed most literally in the obesity of a large proportion of the population. No wonder we are the most overweight, out-of-shape people in the world. Our days are spent sitting at desks, driving our cars, lounging in front of television sets, and sleeping. Children don't even walk to school any more; they are transported by neighborhood car pools. Whenever I suggest to my child that he walk to school, he makes it sound as if I'm ordering him to go on a Paris Island death march. Heaven forbid he should become overheated or out of breath as a result of that grueling three-and-a-half block ordeal each morning. American children lag far behind their European counterparts in the performance of physical fitness tests, and the shocking U. S. Army rejection rate indicates that there is little improvement in later years.

Yet an even more disturbing "softness" is evident—a "softness" of spirit. The frontier was not subdued by the social-security system; the men who crossed the country in covered wagons valued challenge and the chance of finding a better life on the other side of the next mountain far more than security. It was these rugged individuals who made this nation the freest and most powerful in the world; but their success has spoiled us. The drive and determination that was the essence of the American personality has been exchanged for self-contentment and the desire to avoid difficulties. We are going nowhere, and what is worse, we don't seem to care. This, in summary, is the saddening result of thirty years of liberal government.

LIBERAL: If you mean by "soft" that I haven't killed any bears recently or cleared a patch of wilderness for my log cabin, I cannot deny being one of the softest souls alive. But somehow I don't feel terribly guilty about this loss of "ruggedness," primarily because there aren't any bears or wilderness around to conquer. In fact, I seldom even contemplate our loss of old frontiers and ways of life; the demands and challenges of today just do not leave me enough time.

Americans may not be as physically fit as they once were or as trim as the inhabitants of other countries, but this is simply because our technology has provided us with an abundance of material comforts. There are two solutions to this problem: we can either outlaw automobiles, office work, television sets, and other alternatives to strenuous physical activity, or we can exercise more and eat less. To my way of thinking, this latter course makes more sense than trying to return to the days of the horse and buggy, pre-dawn chores, and the corn husk. I find it hard to understand your accusation that liberal government, or any government for that matter, is to blame for the invention of the electric golf cart or the transistor radio, and the subsequent fact that many Americans are overweight. Remember, it all started long ago when some cave man discovered that objects could be moved more easily on stone disks—to which he arbitrarily assigned the name "wheels"—than by being pulled along the ground. This marked the beginning of our physical decline, and it occurred long before writing systems, much less the liberal legislation, had been developed.

I cannot accept the idea that success in this jet age requires less determination and strength of character than was demanded of our pioneering predecessors. Today's struggles and challenges may be different, but they are hardly easier.

Protecting one's family from Indians was undoubtedly not easy, but neither is preventing a world with hydrogen bombs from destroying itself; and scratching a living from the soil entailed no more fortitude and ingenuity than selling soft goods to hostile wholesalers. If anything, twentieth-century man labors under greater pressure and tension than the residents of slower-moving ages.

The difficulties that today's young people face in finding good jobs and finishing the higher education needed to compete in our specialized society require a certain kind of ruggedness, although perhaps not exactly the same as that which you ascribe to the pioneers. And "spiritual softness," whatever you understand the phrase to mean, does not characterize the thousands of young people who have volunteered to spend two years with the Peace Corps building irrigation systems in Iran, for example, or those who are helping to rejuvenate run-down neighborhoods on Chicago's South Side with the War on Poverty's VISTA program.

With the disappearance of the American frontier at the end of the nineteenth century, the day of the Daniel Boones and Davy Crocketts was gone forever. But it was soon evident that the settlement of the West had set in motion new political, economic, and social forces for Americans to conquer. Nature's frontier of wilderness, wild animals, and the elements was already being replaced in the East by a man-made frontier of slums, business slumps, and congestion, which called for "pioneers" with as much courage and ability as those who charted the unknown waters and trails of the land to the west.

Seventy-five years later man is still confronted with enough problems and crises to keep him restive and creative; and as far as I can see, there are no signs that this condition will pass in the very near future.

3
Socialism, states' rights, and the Constitution

Probably the most difficult conservative charge to handle is the accusation that liberalism leads to socialism. This is not because the conservatives have an especially strong case, but because their criticism in this vein is usually vague and hard to define. If the conservative will accept the standard definition of socialism —"government ownership of the means of production"—the liberal can easily point out that federal ownership is very limited and that the government is constantly divesting itself of holdings.

But most conservatives today talk of modern socialism in terms of federal control of the economy through regulation and planning. Since every set of officeholders in our history has intervened in the economy to one extent or another, the question of socialism becomes one of degree. This is why the conservative claim that "we're on the road to socialism" is tricky to pin down.

A convincing liberal reply should therefore incorporate a brief history of federal intervention, a discussion of the contem-

*porary liberal philosophy, the present extent of government reg-
ulation and the justification for that regulation, and a review of
the liberal approach to states' rights and the proper interpretation of the Constitution. This is clearly the most intellectually
challenging conservative argument to break down, and can be
the most rewarding if done successfully.*

• *Since the reign of FDR began, America has been moving rapidly
down the road to socialism.*

CONSERVATIVE: Liberals are always so perplexed when a conservative gets up in Congress and passionately opposes what appears to be a trivial piece of federal legislation. The conservative
involved is usually laughed at by the liberals as a "reactionary"
who has a medieval attitude toward change. "What's all this
hogwash about lost freedom and federal centralization," liberals
ask. "Look around you," they say. "Does the government in
Washington run your lives? Has it seized your businesses and
farms? Of course not. Conservatives just don't understand the
twentieth century, and they fear what they don't understand. In
reality there's nothing to be afraid of; your government is just
helping society adjust to the facts of modern life." I have heard
this liberal line over and over again, and all it demonstrates to
me is that it is the liberals who are still blind to what is happening in America.

No one—except the extreme lunatic fringe, who are not conservatives any more than the Communists on the other fringe are
liberals—says that we are currently a socialist, completely state-
run society. If we were, it would be too late and it would be
useless for the conservative Congressman to speak out against
liberal legislation—that is, if there were still a Congress to speak
in. But liberals walk along with their eyes to the ground, constantly reassuring the rest of us that the path is safe because we
haven't fallen off yet, and never looking to see where the path is

leading. Well, despite your soothing words, some conservatives have raised their eyes from the path, and what they see is liberal government leading this nation straight down the road to state socialism.

By socialism I don't mean the outdated Marxist definition of state ownership of the means of production. People in this country are aware of the dangers of nationalizing industries, and they would never let the government get away with it. The socialism I'm talking about is much more subtle, and for that reason all the more dangerous. The collectivists have discovered that expropriation is not the only way to subordinate the individual and the economy to state control. Taxation and federal regulation do the job just as well, even if they are not as dramatic as an uprising of the proletariat. Socialism in America is coming in a piecemeal fashion, so that no single extension of federal power appears very threatening or alarming. This has been the secret of its success so far.

And it is not as though this process were just getting under way. During a third of a century of liberal domination, the government has been gaining a foothold in nearly every area of national endeavor. The farmer is told what and how much to grow. The businessman is continually harassed by federal rules, regulations, and "guidelines." Standards of health, labor, and education are increasingly set in Washington. The average American now pays out one-third of his earnings in taxes, which is another way of saying that he works one-third of his time for the government, which then takes his money and uses it on people who have done nothing to earn it. As Barry Goldwater said, "By this measure the United States is already one-third 'socialized.' "

Slowly but surely Washington is coming to control the nation's major economic decisions. This is a sure sign that we are approaching the new socialism, a socialism in which the government doesn't demand the deed to our property, only the power to tell us what to do with it. But who can honestly say there is much difference?

Are conservatives frightened? We certainly are, because the

alternatives facing the nation are, on the one hand, a free capitalistic society which values individuality, and on the other, a collective socialist society which demands conformity and subordination. If we don't change direction soon, it is easy to figure out that we're going to end up with the latter. Conservatives keep bringing up this point because they do not believe that most of the people who have voted for a liberal government want socialism; but if these people don't wake up soon to what is going on, they are not going to have any choice in the matter.

LIBERAL: Liberals also see the alternatives of freedom and totalitarianism, of diversity and conformity, facing the nation. If liberals seem to take conservative fears lightly at times, it's only because they view the dangers to our system differently than conservatives do. Conservatives say that America is becoming a socialist state through increased federal intervention, that a trend is evident which—unless something is done to reverse it—will end in government control of everything. If this were the case, I would share your concern, because liberals don't want statism or socialism in this country any more than conservatives do. But I just don't believe a careful study of federal behavior supports your analysis of the situation.

To start with, I think conservatives would be less alarmed by recent government economic intervention if they were more aware of Washington's past role in the development of the country. Federal action to stimulate the economy and provide conditions for growth and progress was not a New Deal innovation, as conservatives often imply. This sort of thing goes back to the early Congresses where men in powdered wigs and knee britches discussed national banks, protective tariffs, and federal spending for internal improvements.

You imply that the use of tax money for public projects is the act of a government creeping toward socialism. Federal funds have been used to build roads, canals, and dams since George Washington's time. When Abraham Lincoln signed the first Pacific Railway Act in 1862, which ultimately committed 155 million acres of public lands and sixty-five million dollars in government loans to subsidize the construction of the transcontinental railroads, was capitalism being abandoned?

You claim that federal regulation of private enterprise is the new liberal strategy for collectivizing the economy. In 1887, Congress passed the Interstate Commerce Act with the expressed purpose of regulating the railroads. Business mergers and other ownership arrangements in restraint of interstate trade were forbidden by the Sherman Antitrust Act of 1890. Federal regulation of railroad rates—which meant that the government could tell a number of businessmen what they could and couldn't charge—was authorized by the 1906 Hepburn Act, whose provisions were later extended to include the telephone and telegraph industries. And the Pure Food and Drug Act of the same year, which forbade certain industrial processing techniques and established health and sanitation standards, is as direct a government intervention as any that has been authorized since 1933. Was it Grover Cleveland, Benjamin Harrison, and Theodore Roosevelt who put us on the road to socialism?

Whenever liberals have mentioned federal monetary controls, labor legislation, and welfare programs in the years since 1933, conservatives have screamed "socialism" and "state control of the individual." Yet back in 1913 the Federal Reserve Board was created to manage our currency and set up safeguards against excessive speculation. Before we got involved in World War I, the Wilson administration passed the Adamson Act to establish an eight-hour day for interstate railroad workers, and a law excluding the products of child labor from interstate commerce.

The point I am trying to make is simply this: Total absence of federal intervention in the economy never existed in this country; and the development of social regulation and controls—which conservatives tend to attribute solely to FDR and his successors—has been going on steadily in both state and national governments since the mid-1880's. If you maintain that increased federal intervention inevitably leads to socialism, at least you should recognize that the country has been moving deliberately in this direction for a good eighty years—half of our history as an independent nation. Your so-called "liberal collectivists" have only been in Washington for three decades.

I think people often lose sight of this because they look at the government economic policies of the 1920's and assume that these were representative of what had always been. But the twenties, far from being a return to the "normalcy" of the pre-World-War-I years, were a reaction to the federal regulation started by the Progressive movement during the late nineteenth century. Once you realize this, you can see that the New Deal really was an attempt to catch up with the reforms that had been cut short by the war and stalled by the reaction of the 1920's. Most of what Roosevelt and his Congresses did was not so new or revolutionary; most of their methods had precedent in American tradition. What made the New Deal seem radical to some people was the scale and speed at which things were done. But given the state of the nation they inherited from conservative management in 1933, liberals did not have much choice. In other words, the New Deal and what has come after it were a continuation of what had been happening more slowly before, not an abrupt swing in a new direction.

CONSERVATIVE: You make it sound as though there was nothing new about the New Deal. I can't remember Theodore Roosevelt ever suggesting a social-security system or a federal dole. But Franklin Roosevelt certainly got us involved with that sort of thing fast enough, and it is this kind of government activity that is socializing the country.

LIBERAL: The demand for economic security had been growing since the depressions of 1873 and 1893, and as I already mentioned, many of the states had responded with legislation. In fact, federal employees were covered by workman's compensation during Theodore Roosevelt's first term in the White House.

With the Great Depression, people were asking for a comprehensive, federal social-insurance system. They were simply unwilling to go through another experience like the one they had suffered in the years right after the Crash—that was one aspect of the old order they just didn't want anymore. Social security didn't restrict people's freedom, or make them dependent on the federal government in any meaningful way. We went through all that earlier in our discussion of individual freedom under liberalism. And Theodore Roosevelt never had to contemplate putting millions of Americans on the dole, because he was never confronted with the unemployment of one-quarter of the labor force.

I do not claim that everything liberals did had been tried before. Unprecedented problems called for original solutions. But the New Deal clearly was not a revolution.

Now let's take a look at the "trend" which frightens you so much. Conservatives are quick to tell us that federal controls and regulations have been increasing steadily over the years. No one takes issue with this. But it is not enough just to point to this increase as though its significance were self-evident. It may mean that we're on the road to socialism and it may not. We cannot know until we examine the reasons for this increasing government centralization and intervention, and the effects it has had.

Do you know who said this? "The great development of industrialism means that there must be an increase in the supervision exercised by the Government over business enterprise."

Sound like Roosevelt? It was—Theodore Roosevelt. He said it in 1905. Was he contemplating the need for a socialist society? It's much more likely that he had realized, as had so many very unradical politicians around the turn of the century, that American capitalism had some serious deficiencies that needed repair if it were going to survive. Competition had been replaced in many industries by monopolies and trusts. This may have come about in a free market, but its result was to destroy the functioning of that market. It was pretty meaningless to say consumers were free to choose between different brands when these brands were all managed by the same holding company. The same was true for wages. If a steel worker could only work for one corporation or for several corporations with agreements to keep wages at one low level, the idea that the forces of supply and demand were determining what he earned was nonsense—the owners of that corporation or group of corporations working together dictated his pay check.

In this situation, the government was confronted with several alternatives. It could ignore what was happening and allow a small number of industrialists to set prices and wages in each industry. But, in practice, this was hardly compatible with the general welfare of the population, and the resulting economy certainly wasn't capitalism as America had known it.

On the other hand, the government could decide that since competition didn't exist anymore, it would be better to have people managing industry who at least were responsible to the voters, and that the wisest course would be to nationalize our economy. This would have been the socialist solution.

Theodore Roosevelt and his contemporaries chose a middle road, which in the truest sense of the word was a "conservative" course. They believed that private enterprise was a valuable safeguard of individual freedom and that it had the potential to provide the American people with an efficient, expanding, and responsive economy. But—and this is an important "but"—they also realized that private enterprise could be preserved *only* if the government accepted the responsibility of maintaining competition wherever possible and intervened to maintain a just balance between business, labor, and the consumer whenever the market could not do so. Industrialization and new business practices—not the federal government—had changed the U.S. economy. But it fell to Washington to find a way of sustaining private enterprise in a form acceptable to the American people. And the cost of this decision to "conserve" our capitalistic system was limited government controls and regulation of business.

There are lots of other reasons why government has been

forced to expand so much in the twentieth century. To start with, there are presently four times as many people to govern as there were, say, in 1880. More important, at that date only nine million people lived in cities, whereas 130 million live in them today. City living means direct contact between people and great social and economic interdependence. When Americans were scattered across the continent on small, largely self-sufficient farms, they didn't need garbage collection, elaborate police and fire departments, zoning codes, mass transit systems, public recreation facilities, slum-clearance programs, and the thousand-and-one other public services required by today's urban dwellers. This increase and shift in the population automatically meant enormously expanded state and local governments; and when some services became too large and expensive for these governments to handle alone, the federal government had to step in and help.

More federal intervention is also necessary today because the economy has become increasingly interstate and international during the century. The larger corporations have plants all over the country and in some cases throughout the world. In response to this development, labor unions have organized on a national basis. In such an economy, only a national government can be expected to deal with problems in a comprehensive and effective manner.

Furthermore, more things need doing today that are either too big for private enterprise or that aren't profitable in a commercial sense. Conservation is a good example. By the time Theodore Roosevelt became president, there was already a recognition that something had to be done to rescue and rehabilitate America's national resources—her croplands, forests, mineral wealth, and waters. You couldn't expect anyone but the government to be interested in this sort of large-scale, long-range project. In 1933 only eleven percent of the nation's farms had electricity. The reason private power companies weren't supplying rural electricity was that to service a lot of widely scattered farms would require a tremendous outlay in lines and other equipment.

To make it profitable, rates would have to be so high that most farmers just couldn't afford it. This is why FDR called for the creation of the Rural Electrification Administration as the only way the countryside could be electrified. Washington also moved increasingly into the spotlight as the United States became a world power with large defense needs and commitments around the globe. Clearly, foreign affairs and defense are federal responsibilities.

In short, all government, and particularly federal government, has intervened to a greater degree in the life of the country because population changes, a more advanced economy, and our new position in world affairs have demanded it. A refusal to act would have jeopardized the very democratic and economic institutions Americans wanted to preserve.

CONSERVATIVE: I conceded earlier that most liberals believe there is good reason for government centralization. I'm not questioning motives, but rather the effects of all this new federal power and control of the economy. The fact is that, step by step, Washington has become the nation's major economic decision-maker; and if this process is allowed to go much further, this is going to be a socialist country with all of the attendant evils.

LIBERAL: I agree that intentions are not enough, that it is results that count. So let's look at results. Capitalism operates on the principles of competition, while socialism is committed to the elimination of competition. Whether our economy has become more or less competitive with increased government intervention ought to be a good test of where we're going.

Historically, the earliest federal actions to regulate business were aimed at restoring the competition that the monopolies and trusts were destroying. Over the last seventy-five years the Justice Department has broken up and prevented numerous business combinations and arrangements that were anticompetitive.

These efforts, in which liberals have played a key role, have resulted in the replacement of the effective monopolies which were so common at the turn of the century with oligopolies—the domination of an industry by a few large, competing firms. While businessmen as a group have always praised free competition as vital to the well-being of a capitalist system, individual owners have too often succumbed to the understandably tempting alternative of cooperation and collusion. It's sort of ironic that, for the past three-quarters of a century, it has been the federal government that has been forced to struggle against much of the business community to keep private enterprise competitive in America. Mind you, there's still a lot left to be done. Price competition in the automobile and steel industries is nonexistent, just to name two cases; but we're making some progress. So here you see our economy's competitiveness increasing, not diminishing, under liberal government.

Liberals have promoted competition by lowering the record high tariffs of the twenties and allowing more foreign products into the country. They also work to make competition more honest. If products do not do what their manufacturers claim they do, or if they are packaged and labeled deceptively, consumers can't make rational decisions as to what is the best buy for their money. By enforcing honest packaging and labeling, liberals have protected honest businessmen against those who might use unfair methods.

Now that I think about it, I don't know of a single federal action since 1933 to reduce competition that wasn't taken at the request of businessmen themselves. Projects like the TVA actually strengthen real rate competition. In short, if the degree of competition is any indication of what kind of economy a country has, the U.S. economy has been moving *away* from socialism for the last thirty-three years.

You also claimed that liberal government has been gradually depriving businessmen of the power to make the important decisions in running their enterprises, and that this is the modern way of socializing an economy. Offhand, I can think of eight basic decisions which businessmen traditionally have had to make. First, they have to decide what goods or services they want to sell. Now aside from a few items like heroin and germ-warfare kits for children, a person is free to manufacture almost anything he can think of. The only significant role the federal government plays here is to undertake billions of dollars worth of research—amounting to one-sixth of the entire government budget—much of which results in new products for private firms to produce and market. Then there is the question of how much to produce. With the exception of agriculture, which is a special case we can take up later, there are no federal restrictions in this area.

The businessman also decides how he will produce his goods or services. The government does nothing about how goods are manufactured, except for setting minimal health and safety standards. When it comes to financing an enterprise, the federal government does intervene. If a firm wants to issue stocks or bonds, it has to make application for approval to the Securities and Exchange Commission. This is to insure full disclosure of all relevant information, to prevent reckless speculation, and to rule out the possibility of tips and other special advantages to insiders. The result of these regulations has been to restore public confidence in the securities market, which had been badly deflated and discredited by the Crash of '29. Twenty million Americans hold stocks today. This unprecedented confidence in the market has meant cheaper borrowing rates for businessmen. In short, it's never been easier for firms to finance their ventures.

Then there are decisions involving wages and labor relations. Here the government has intervened to see that labor and management meet on terms as close to equality as possible, and federal regulations set minimum wages and maximum hours which apply to all businesses in interstate trade. But, besides this lower limit on wages—$1.25 an hour, or $2,600 a year for a man working a forty-hour week, fifty-two weeks a year—businessmen and their employees are left to themselves to work out wages, working conditions, and fringe benefits.

Another big decision is how much to charge for goods and services. There are federal controls over the rates of public utilities and certain portions of the transportation industry—some of which were requested by the industries—but all other businesses are left to set prices as they please.

The furious activity on Madison Avenue and the new advertising gimmicks and slogans that appear every year ought to be ample evidence that the question of how to sell products remains very much with the businessman. This only leaves the problem of where to sell products. Americans cannot market their output in Red China, North Korea, North Vietnam, or Cuba, and strategic materials are barred from the other Communist bloc countries. But aside from these restrictions, an individual can sell anywhere in the United States and any place else that foreign governments permit. In fact, the Commerce and State departments help American businessmen locate new markets and expand existing ones.

These are the controls and regulations which you contend are steadily socializing the U.S. economy. When you take a look at what the federal government actually does, it becomes clear that, while Washington does rule out certain commercial alternatives viewed as harmful to business, employees, consumers, or the economy as a whole, this is a far cry from the government's assuming the responsibility for making fundamental business decisions. As you can see, the meaningful alternatives are still selected by the businessman and nobody else.

CONSERVATIVE: And what about government planning?

LIBERAL: In this country there just isn't any direct economic planning of the comprehensive type; that is, the type where businesses are instructed by a government agency how much to produce, what prices to charge, and what wages to pay. The National Recovery Administration (NRA) toyed with some of these ideas during the Depression, but this approach to the economy was abandoned as unworkable and undesirable even before the NRA was declared unconstitutional.

But we do have federal policies for planned economic growth.

The relevant question to ask here is: Planned growth for whom? The beneficiary of this planning is private enterprise.

Take the tax cut. It produced economic expansion with no strings attached. People bought what they wanted with the extra income that resulted from reduced taxes, and businessmen responded to this new consumer demand and the cut in corporate taxes as they saw fit. The government did not intervene at any point. In fact, in recent years the private sector of the economy has been expanding at a much faster rate than the public sector, which is a rather roundabout way of "creeping toward socialism." For that matter, how do you explain a tax cut by a government that you say is socializing the country through taxation?

CONSERVATIVE: Now you're the one who is being inconsistent. You admit that liberals have increased government intervention in the economy, but you vehemently deny that this is leading us to socialism. Pray tell then, where is it leading?

LIBERAL: Liberals hope it is leading to an improvement in America's democratic, mixed-capitalist society. Also, you seem to forget that it often takes a lot of action just to maintain what you've got—just to stand still.

Liberals think that the concept of very limited government, which was workable in the eighteenth century and much of the nineteenth century, is no longer feasible. Besides, the majority of Americans have made it obvious that they do not want to return to a modified laissez-faire political philosophy. On the other hand, liberals want to avoid the other extreme of a state-run economy or socialism. So, despite strong pressures during the Depression from the far left and right to abandon our private enterprise economy for government ownership or absolute controls, liberals committed the federal government to a policy of preserving our basic democratic and economic institutions. Accomplishing this has involved discarding parts of the system that weren't performing what was expected of them and adding parts which were demanded by new realities. However, the crucial point to remember is that these changes have all been *within* our traditional system, with the aim of keeping it workable.

A third of a century later, it seems to me that this "conservative" course liberals have been following since 1933 is working. Private enterprise is thriving. The private sector of the economy is steadily increasing as a proportion of the national economy. The prestige of the businessman in this country has been restored to its pre-Crash level or even higher. At the same time we are keeping democracy functioning and providing reasonably well for our national needs. So I find no evidence to indicate that we should change our system—either now or in the foreseeable future—to one of comprehensive government management of the economy. Our middle course is working well. We will continue our efforts to maintain a viable, expanding, private enterprise system in America.

• *Liberal principles and programs are just a mask for socialist ideas.*

CONSERVATIVE: You claim that you don't want socialism in America any more than conservatives do; that you're trying to steer some middle course short of state control of the economy. Have you ever looked to see where the guiding principles and major programs of contemporary liberalism come from? They're socialist in origin. This whole business about government centralization, regulating the economy, and redistributing wealth— which is what your "progressive" income tax does—comes straight out of the writings of the British Fabian socialists.

Liberals apparently regard their actions as isolated attempts to solve specific problems within the capitalist system. Actually, liberal programs and policies are individual components of a comprehensive socialist blueprint for a radically new economy and society. Read some of the writings of the Webbs, George Bernard Shaw, and the other British collectivists. They weren't interested in keeping English private enterprise afloat. They knew that the chances of pulling off a revolution were nonexistent, so to build a socialist state they advocated a piecemeal approach that gave the appearance of having no purpose beyond the random strengthening of established institutions. Their proposals seemed haphazard—this was their intention. But they had a very definite goal in mind, namely, socialism in England. From our vantage point a half-century later, we can see just how successful this strategy was.

What surprises me—I'm still assuming that most liberals don't want socialism—is that you have been taken in by this transparent maneuver. By using socialist sources for ideas and programs, liberals are putting together a society in which the federal government will ultimately control the economy and the individual. If you really want to know where liberalism leads, look at a country that has been governed by these same principles; look at Britain and the direction it's taking. Then perhaps it will be clear to you that, for the last thirty-three years, America has been traveling the road to socialism.

LIBERAL: That's a very imaginative thesis. But you won't find much support for it in U.S. history. The liberal principles and programs of the New Deal and the Great Society trace their roots to the plains of drought-stricken Kansas, to the tenant farms of Georgia, to the slums of Chicago, and to the universities and clubs of the East—not to the coffee houses of London. Contemporary liberalism, whatever else you can say of it, is as American as Coca-Cola.

In the first place, you've got your chronology turned around. The reform movement of the late nineteenth century, of which liberalism is a continuation, was well under way before the Fabian socialists were known outside of Britain. The farmers of the Midwest and South, who started the first rumblings of discontent and disillusionment with Washington's hands-off policy, had no access to the pamphlets of Sidney Webb or the plays and essays of George Bernard Shaw. Americans who were demanding change were moved by the conditions that confronted them. If any ideology played a part, it was the Jeffersonian vision of effective democracy and a chance for the "little man." Later, people may have picked up doctrines from abroad to give the growing protest some form, but, for the most part, such ideological considerations and political labels were after the fact.

As you pointed out earlier, the nineteenth century saw the United States grow from thirteen weak, quarreling colonies into the leading industrial nation of the world. But all this progress had come at a price. In the process of conquering the continent, the soil, forests, and waters had been exploited. Agriculture had grown tremendously, yet by the 1880's and 1890's the farmer was on the verge of ruin. Our successful industrial revolution had been accompanied by inhumane, unhealthy working conditions, child labor, the business cycle with its depressions and mass unemployment, insecurity in old age, and poor treatment of the incompetent and infirm. The new wealth of the nation was piling up in fewer and fewer hands; estimates indicate that in 1890, one-eighth of the population owned seven-eighths of the wealth. Urbanization had led to the development of slums like those in Europe, and millions of people lived in extreme want. Negroes were still second-class citizens in both the North and the South, a full generation after the Civil War. And many governmental units that could have worked to correct these conditions were mired in graft and corruption.

The men and women who decided that reform was desperately needed were not inspired by socialist tracts or bearded conspirators; they simply looked around and didn't like what they saw. People read utopian novels such as Edward Bellamy's *Looking Backward,* which gave them a picture of what an "ideal" collective society might be like, but the social politics in these books never really caught on.

Now let me point out who *were* the actual forerunners of the New Deal. A good place to start is with the so-called "agrarian revolt." After the Civil War, American farmers began to complain about what they considered unfair practices by the railroads. They also believed that the scarcity of money outside the East led to high interest rates and undue hardship for Western borrowers. In time, this scattered and incoherent rural protest grew into the Populist movement. Under the leadership of such picturesque characters as Pitchfork Ben Tillman, Sockless Jerry Simpson, Ignatius Donnelly, Mary "raise-less-coin-and-more-hell" Lease, and the boy orator from Nebraska, William Jennings Bryan—a group that had about as much in common with the Fabians as Andrew Jackson had with Karl Marx—the Populists gained massive support throughout the farm lands of the South, Midwest, and Plains States in the opening years of the 1890's.

Were they interested in making America socialist? On the contrary, the Populists were trying to recapture an earlier America in which the common man—which to them meant the small farmer—was able to compete economically and to have a voice in government. Their guiding light, to the extent they had one, was Thomas Jefferson. Far from advocating the subordination of the individual to the state, they fought, as William Jennings Bryan put it, for "anything that makes the government more democratic, more popular in form, anything that gives the people more control of the government."

If you want further evidence of their intentions, take a look at the platform drafted at the Populist Party convention in Omaha in 1882. Labeled "communistic" by some people, the platform called for such "collectivist measures" as postal savings banks, a graduated income tax, the free and unlimited coinage of silver, a flexible currency controlled by the government, a sub-treasury system, an eight-hour day for labor, the direct election of senators, and the right of citizens to initiate laws and pass on others by referendum. The platform also demanded government ownership of the railroads, not because the Populists desired a state-contolled economy, but because they felt the railroads were killing private agriculture; it was either the railroads or the farmers as they saw it. Within a generation, almost every one of these planks had become law, in whole or in part. Populism, which the historians Morison and Commager called "the seedbed of American politics for the next half-century," was dedicated to strengthening democracy and making private enterprise work, not just for the powerful and wealthy, but for everyone.

During the Populist days, the cities might well have provided fertile soil for socialist ideas. A series of depressions with severe unemployment, starting with the Panic of 1873, had brought a growing unrest which was beginning to find a new channel of expression: the labor union. For the first time, labor unions were a serious topic among large numbers of American workers. And since unions were the best organized element of the urban protest, it was logical for the socialists to concentrate their efforts here.

A few radicals in the unions taught the class warfare and proletarian politics of Karl Marx. Others advocated a domestic brand of socialism, telling the worker that he would never find justice under capitalism and that the exploited laboring masses must unite to change the system democratically through the ballot box. In 1896, the Socialist Labor Party ran a candidate for president who received about 30,000 votes.

But, for all their efforts, the socialists were never able to get their primary objectives accepted by the majority of working men. The people who worked in the nation's factories, railroads, and mines were not as interested in a classless society as they were in finding a place for themselves in the middle class. They didn't object to capitalism, but to their own "raw deal"—not a large enough share of the profits. The cause that sent nearly a half-million working men into the streets and led to the bloody Haymarket Square riot wasn't the overthrow of private enterprise but the eight-hour day.

The most influential union during this hectic period was Samuel Gompers' American Federation of Labor. The epitome of "bread-and-butter" unionism, the AF of L ignored the utopian escapes and cure-alls which had tempted its predecessors and concentrated on organization and collective bargaining. Gompers and his followers accepted capitalism and chose to work within the framework of the existing economic order. Like those of the Populists, their proposals are the best clue to their purposes. They championed the eight-hour day and the six-day week, factory inspection, workmen's compensation, the abolition of child labor, the initiative, referendum, and recall, free schools, free textbooks, and compulsory education.

This list should give you an idea of the kind of impact the labor movement has had on contemporary liberalism. Probe as you will, while you will find plenty of socialists involved with the unions, you will be hard put to it to discover much socialism.

As the century closed, the cry for reform grew louder in city and countryside. During the 1890's, the Populists had won control of the legislatures in several rural states and enacted parts of their platform. But in the big cities, labor wasn't strong enough to dislodge the political bosses. And the federal government, except for a few token moves, remained unresponsive to the swelling mandate for change. It was left to the Progressives of the new century to transform this protest into action at the municipal and national levels.

The Progressives were the least vulnerable to socialism of all of liberalism's predecessors. Coming from families of old wealth and high social standing—the closest the country had to an aristocracy—these new reformers approached the nation's problems with a moral fervor reminiscent of the New England Puritans. They became suddenly afraid that corrupt politics, the desperate condition of many urban dwellers, the lack of industrial competition, and the increasing economic chaos would combine to destroy our democratic and capitalistic institutions. Even more than the farmers and workers, the Progressives were opposed to radical change. The administrative reforms, the fight against bossism, and the regulation of business which they wrote into law in the first fifteen years of this century, were conceived as measures to conserve "the American way of life."

Their most prominent leaders—Bryan, who had made the transition from Populism, Robert La Follette, Theodore Roosevelt, and Woodrow Wilson—viewed their goal as the restoration of lost freedoms: freedom of competition for small business, freedom from the monopolistic control of prices for the con-

sumer, freedom from industrial feudalism for labor, and freedom from dishonest government for everyone. They never lost
their faith in democracy and private enterprise. There was none
of the tendency so evident in Europe to gain order at the cost of
liberty, to substitute an "efficient" dictatorship for ineffective
popular government. The Progressive solution to America's
difficulties was always more democracy. Progressives cam-
paigned for woman's suffrage, the secret ballot, direct election of
senators, the initiative, referendum and recall, municipal home
rule, and government regulation of railroads, utilities, labor,
banking, and finance. Recognizing that much of the corruption
in politics came from the inability of the old administrative
structure to cope with new problems, they championed civil-
service reform, the regulation of campaign expenditures, tax reform, and the commission and the city-manager plans for municipal government. The departure from a government hands-off
policy during this period and the increase in federal centralization reflected not disillusionment with liberty, but new confidence in a more democratically-controlled government.

This was the philosophic and legislative legacy inherited by
the New Deal, the Fair Deal, the New Frontier, and the Great
Society. The Progressive's goal of maintaining democracy and
private enterprise by replacing those parts of the system that
break down has been kept intact by the liberals of recent years.

By the time the New Deal was under way, events in Europe
had made it clear to Franklin Roosevelt that economic insecurity
could cause people to trade democracy for totalitarian certainty.
Believing that a democratic nation could offer its citizens reasonable protection against long-term unemployment, disability,
and poverty in old age, he urged the establishment of a social-
insurance program. This led to the Social Security Act of 1935.

Since World War II, liberals have continued to develop the
principles and programs pioneered by the Populists, the labor
unions, and the Progressives—all of whom believed that government in a democracy should be used as needed, to promote economic growth and individual security.

So my answer to your charge that American liberalism has its foundations in British socialism is simply that the Fabians had almost no influence on our liberal thought and practice. While certain specifics may appear in the platforms of both the British socialists and the American liberals, there are many crucial proposals and goals which they have never shared, such as the nationalization of key industries and government determination of wages and prices. To conclude that our development will parallel Britain's just because both nations have adopted certain similar measures is to ignore important differences in the two programs and the greatly dissimilar economic situations of the two societies.

In short, contemporary American liberalism rose from the desire of earlier generations to expand the opportunity of participation in our democracy and to keep private enterprise thriving. To say that this course must lead to state control of the economy and the subordination of the individual to the government is almost to accuse the framers of the Constitution of socialist intentions! If America should some day become socialist, it will not be because of anything inherent in liberal philosophy. If we can remain on the middle road we are presently traveling, liberals can take considerable credit for trying to find a way between an "all" and a "nothing" approach to government.

• *"Government planning" and "government regulation" are just other names for state control and socialism.*

CONSERVATIVE: You admit that federal planning and regulation of the economy have increased enormously under liberal government. Then, in the same breath, you deny that Washington is coming to control the economy. Obviously, both of these statements can't be true. What is control if it's not regulations and plans imposed by an outside force?

This contradiction completely undermines your argument that liberalism doesn't necessarily lead to socialism. As long as you maintain that federal regulation and planning are essential elements of the liberal philosophy—that is, as long as liberals remain liberals—liberalism must continue to promote government control of the economy. This is the basis of the new socialism. As I said earlier, liberalism is a means of collectivizing a nation gradually instead of abruptly as the Marxists prescribe. One way is slower than the other and more difficult to see, but the results are identical.

You are caught on the horns of a lethal dilemma. Either you renounce economic intervention—which is the major distinguishing factor between liberals and conservatives—or you must concede that your political philosophy is leading America into socialism. No matter which alternative you choose, liberalism ceases to be what you claim it is.

LIBERAL: Federal regulation and planning do involve controls, but we cannot just stop there and conclude that socialism is therefore just around the corner. There are different kinds of controls. For example, drivers are not allowed to exceed twenty-five miles an hour on certain streets; to that extent they are controlled by city statute. We distinguish this situation from one in which these same laws might specify when and where people may drive. If we are going to talk about control in the broad sense you suggest, we should determine the nature and extent of the regulations and the planning in question. Then we can assess their consequences.

In a socialist society, regulation and planning are comprehensive. The government makes all the fundamental economic decisions: what is produced, how much is produced, how it is marketed, how it is financed, what prices are charged for goods and services, and what wages are paid to labor. Any private prerogatives are exceptions to the rule and subject to the state's discretion.

By contrast, liberal governments in this country have never sought to run the economy; the regulation and planning undertaken since 1933 have been of a very different kind than those used by the socialists. The basic business decisions I outlined above have been left in private hands. As you recall, I talked about these decisions and the liberal legislation affecting them at the beginning of our discussion of socialism (on p. 71). Most federal regulations were written with the same intent as our traffic regulations: to set limits on certain private activities and to prevent practices that our elected representatives consider dangerous or unfair. Antitrust laws, packaging requirements, and the minimum wage have eliminated some economic alternatives; but the vast range of important choices confronting business, labor, and the consumer have remained untouched. Unlike the socialists, liberals accept private enterprise as the dominant force in the American economy. The regulation and planning of the New Deal and the programs since then have been aimed at strengthening the private sector by helping it adjust to changing conditions.

To say that increased federal intervention is leading us to state control of the economy and socialism is to ignore the kinds of situations in which the government has intervened. The telling question is: Are these regulations leading to federal control of the big economic decisions or are they designed to buttress our system of private enterprise?

We think it is very clear that the latter is the case. The limited experiments with production, wage, and price controls of earlier years were totally abandoned. The efforts of the National Recovery Administration to promote industrial cooperation and planning were dropped as unworkable, as well as unconstitutional. Price and wage controls instituted during World War II were quickly dispensed with at the war's end. For a third of a century, liberals have declared their intentions openly and often: Federal regulation and planning are to preserve private enterprise, not to replace it.

If you still insist that intervention is just a euphemism for creeping socialism, you must show exactly how this intervention is taking the economy out of private hands. Frankly, I don't think you'll find it easy.

CONSERVATIVE: What about these things called "federal guide-lines"? When the president wants to regulate something over which the law doesn't give him control, he just issues a "guide-line." At least in socialist countries they regulate by law.

LIBERAL: Government guidelines are only suggested formulas. They propose price and wage changes which the president believes will promote the growth and stability of the economy. They have always been voluntary.

CONSERVATIVE: I don't agree that they're voluntary. What about President Kennedy's intervention in the steel industry a couple of years ago? If you want proof that government interference is synonymous with real control of the economy, there it is.

LIBERAL: The steel affair does prove an important point, but not quite the one you suggest. Let's review the sequence of events.

Following the federal guidelines proposed for the steel industry, the United Steel Workers had tacitly agreed to limit their wage demands if management would give its word that steel prices would be raised by only a certain amount. The promise was made; labor followed through and signed a contract calling for minimal wage increases. Almost immediately, contrary to their agreement, the United States Steel Corporation announced a sizeable price hike. At this point, President Kennedy informed the voters that the corporation had betrayed the trust of the steel workers and that, in his opinion, the proposed price increase would promote inflation and be contrary to the best interests of the nation. U. S. Steel reconsidered its decision and ultimately raised prices by a smaller amount.

President Kennedy's attempt to mobilize public opinion against the price hike raised a great storm of criticism in the business community. It marked a peril point of action which Kennedy, and President Johnson after him, carefully refrained from approaching again. Guidelines have continued but, in the attempt to have them observed, presidents have not used a heavy hand.

If the Kennedy incident had set a precedent for subsequent unlimited federal intervention, your argument would have some weight. But the fact that the President and everyone involved recognized that he had overstepped the limits of voluntary cooperation pretty well demolishes your contention that federal regulation is the forerunner of socialism.

• *Once the government gets its foot in the door somewhere, it's only a matter of time until it takes over that area completely.*

CONSERVATIVE: Your claim that liberalism doesn't necessarily lead to socialism reminds me of the classic definition of a liberal as a person who believes it's possible to be a little bit pregnant. You assume that a government can rest satisfied with "just a little regulation here and a little control there to keep the economy running smoothly." This may hold up all right in theory, but in the real world things don't work that way.

Past experience has repeatedly shown that some political power invariably breeds a lust for more political power. It is unfortunate but true that man's appetite cannot be satisfied until he has complete control over a situation. Translated into federal regulation of the economy, this means that once the government gets its foot in the door in a given area of private activity, it is only a matter of time before the government takes that area over. No matter how much you declare that a government-run economy is contrary to liberal principles and intentions, liberals are only men and they must be expected to act accordingly. While conservatives have always taken human frailties into consideration in pondering the proper role of the state, liberals constantly delude themselves into thinking that somehow they will avoid man's historic weaknesses. This vanity—for there is no other word for it—has made them blind to the consequences of the liberal philosophy.

Conservatives have been sounding this warning since 1933, and liberal actions have only substantiated it. Look at the nation's air lines. A number of years ago, the federal government decided to help the commercial aviation industry get off the ground. Perhaps there was nothing wrong with this initial decision, but federal money always has strings attached. Today, the Civil Aeronautics Board dictates flight routes and schedules, passenger and freight rates, the type of planes used, pilot licensing, safety regulations, and even the kind of food that air lines may serve you for lunch! What began as a helping hand has turned into complete government control. Far from being an exception, this pattern of federal intervention has been evident in industry after industry.

Our choice is simple. Since governments consist of mortal men and not saints, limited government regulation of the economy cannot last long. Either we must act quickly to return Washington to its proper place or we must accept the inevitability of socialism in America.

LIBERAL: During World War II, the U.S. government built billions of dollars worth of defense plants. In the years since V-J Day, these plants have been sold to private interests and the nation's defense needs have been contracted out to private firms. At one time U.S. mail was delivered on Air Force planes; now this job is handled by the commercial air lines. Price and rent controls were in effect for part of the war and the immediate post-war period; but, as soon as reconversion was reasonably well advanced, these controls were dropped. When Congress passed the Social Security Act in 1935, critics screamed that the entire insurance industry would soon be government-owned; since then, the private insurance companies have grown faster than ever. There are plenty of cases in which federal regulation of an industry has been steadily expanded over the years, but I can cite an equal number in which government economic intervention has remained static, or diminished, or totally disappeared. The oft-repeated conservative charge that one regulation inevitably leads to another is a lot of hogwash.

When a regulation becomes law, its supporters are usually satisfied for a time, and not interested in putting up a fight for further controls. At the same time, those who opposed the initial measure can be expected to offer even stiffer resistance to additional regulation. This common political phenomenon was one of the reasons liberals encountered so much difficulty in enacting their medicare proposal. The original Social Security Act passed easily because a vast majority of Americans felt the need for some kind of social-insurance system. Drafted in 1935 by the Roosevelt administration, the act was passed the same year. By contrast, the Murray-Wagner-Dingell bill, calling for a national health-insurance program financed through social security, was first introduced in 1943. Twenty-two years later, after exhaustive debate and vigorous opposition by private interest groups, Congress passed a limited plan to provide hospitalization costs for the elderly under social security. This fell far short of the original proposal for a program to cover all of the medical expenses of every American regardless of age, a program which may never be realized. So, instead of one intervention paving the way for the next, the first often diminishes the following one's chances of success.

Time and again in this discourse, you have implied that public officials operate in a realm beyond the reach of ordinary people. Even if every bureaucrat in Washington is as "power-mad" as you suggest—and who's to judge?—I don't see that this would matter much. Whenever the head of a federal regulatory commission declares that a new governmental power is required, whatever his motives, he must petition our popularly-elected Congress for the authority to act. If Congress refuses to grant that authority, all his craving for power will not make that regulation a reality. If our elected representatives do agree that additional government controls are advisable, the American people can reject their judgment at the next election. A little more confidence in our democratic processes would go a long way toward calming your fears about possible federal excesses.

CONSERVATIVE: But you do admit that one federal regulation has led to others in many areas?

LIBERAL: No, one hasn't led to another; one has sometimes been followed by another. There's a difference. Congress doesn't reason that a new control should be passed just because a precedent has been set. Additional regulations are established in an area either when the previous ones didn't fully remedy a situation or when a substantial change of conditions has created new problems.

The air-line industry which you referred to a moment ago illustrates this point. This industry is the most completely regulated business in the country, as you pointed out. But notice what is happening in its relation to government. At the beginning, the government not only regulated but subsidized the industry, paying its operating deficit and making big loans for the purchase of planes. Many people shook their heads and said it was only a question of time before the government took over completely. What happened? The air line companies did a good job of operating their lines. They made a profit and dispensed with government subsidies. On the strength of their prospects, the companies have been able to borrow billions of dollars from the banks for new planes. Today, their future never looked brighter, and private ownership of the industry was never more secure. The regulations still continue and probably always will, but I challenge you to read into them anything sinister.

As I tried to point out in our discussion of freedom (p. 10), government intervention is a method of exchange. Something is given up and something else is received in return. Federal regulation of the aviation industry can only be evaluated by measuring what was gained against what was lost. And if you will take the time to apply this yardstick to the many government interventions in the economy since 1933, I think you will find that the country has come out considerably ahead.

Your contention that socialism is inevitable in this country because limited federal intervention cannot be maintained, simply isn't sound. It ignores the checks and balances in our government, the democratic powers of the people, and the evidence put before us during a third of a century of liberal performance.

• *Liberal disregard of the Constitution and denial of the rights of sovereign states have made federal control of the individual and the economy inevitable.*

CONSERVATIVE: Checks and balances may have protected us a third of a century ago. But today liberals have subverted our single greatest check against concentration of power in Washington: the principle of states' rights. And in the process, the Constitution has been so distorted that the very cornerstone of the republic, our commitment to government by laws and not by men, has begun to crumble. Of all my indictments of liberalism, these are the most profound. Once we abandon our federal system and our faith in constitutionalism, nothing stands between the American people and totalitarianism.

The Tenth Amendment to the Constitution clearly states:

The powers not delegated to the United States by the Constitution nor prohibited by it to the States, are reserved to the States respectively, or to the people.

The framers didn't draw a distinct line between federal and state jurisdiction just to be obstreperous or to make the country hard to govern. They realized that a federal system would be an effective, built-in check against a dangerous centralization of power. By declaring specific areas off limits to the federal government, they assured both decentralization and limited government. They knew, too, that local officials are better suited to deal with essentially local problems.

These reasons for maintaining states' rights are as valid today as they were in 1789. Yet liberals have chosen to disregard them. Beginning with the New Deal, a dramatic shift of power from the city halls and state capitols to Washington has destroyed the balance of duties prescribed by the Constitution. Not content to expand its proper responsibilities to an enormous size, the federal government has increasingly trespassed into the domain of the states.

This centralization of power and usurpation of states' rights has been accomplished in several ways. One of the most effective means has been Washington's seizure of the lion's share of the nation's tax revenue. In 1932, federal spending accounted for one-third of all government expenditures in this country. Today, that figure stands at two-thirds. Obviously, control of a welfare program or a public facility rests with the provider, who, as you can see, is usually the federal government.

Another effective power device is the policy of "grants-in-aid," used by Washington to gain entry into areas from which it is excluded by the Constitution. These grants, called "matching funds," are designed to "stimulate" state spending in health, education, welfare, conservation, or any other area in which federal officials decide there is a "need" for action. At first glance, the states may appear to be getting a bargain, but nothing could be further from the truth.

In the first place, these programs are federal in origin—their scope and objectives are determined in Washington. Second, the states almost have to participate whether they want the programs or not. To refuse, a state must turn down its fair share of money which was collected from all of the states, a decision that's almost certain political suicide for state legislators. What these grants-in-aid actually amount to is a device for coercing the states to foot part of the bill for federal programs.

Finally, the federal government has tightened its hold on the states through the blatantly unconstitutional practice of threatening to do a state's job for it unless the state's performance meets with Washington's approval. This is no idle threat. The most publicized incident of this kind was the Supreme Court's 1954 ruling that the states must desegregate all public schools. Now, the Constitution at no point requires the states to maintain racially-mixed schools; in fact, it invests the federal government with no powers regarding education. The Tenth Amendment reserves jurisdiction over education to the states. The Supreme Court skirted this clear prohibition of federal intervention by invoking the "equal protection" clause of the Fourteenth Amendment. But no one, including the Court, has ever argued that the authors of this amendment intended it to cover education. In fact, all available evidence points to the contrary. Mind you, I personally favor integrated schools. But I don't see that it's my right—or the federal government's—to impose this view on the people of Alabama or Mississippi. As Barry Goldwater said, "The problem of race relations, like all social and cultural problems, is best handled by the people directly concerned."

Whenever I mention to a liberal this steady federal encroachment on states' rights, I usually receive the same tired answer: that states' rights ought to be respected *unless,* in the opinion of federal officials, the states fail to respond "to the needs of the people." States have responsibilities as well as rights; if a state neglects its responsibilities, the argument runs, it defaults its rights to the federal government and has no one to blame but itself for the loss of power.

As you can see, the liberal-conservative disagreement over the meaning of states' rights is no minor academic difference. The interpretation that prevails will determine, in a large part, the future of freedom in America. Liberals obviously believe that government by men may be substituted for government by law whenever Washington chooses. If this isn't a formula for totalitarianism, I've never heard one.

In contrast, conservatives continue to point out that the Tenth Amendment specifies certain areas which belong exclusively to the states. In these areas the states have the prerogative to act or not act, as they see fit. The key factor here, which Barry Goldwater emphasized, is that "the States may have duties corresponding to these rights, but the duties are owed to the people of the States, not to the federal government. Therefore, the recourse lies not with the federal government, which is not sovereign, but with the people who are, and who have full power to take disciplinary action."

LIBERAL: If liberal actions have been as clearly unconstitutional as you claim, why hasn't the Supreme Court intervened to halt them? After all, the Court has the final word in this country as to what violates the Constitution and what doesn't.

CONSERVATIVE: The answer is simply that a liberal Supreme Court has consistently ignored the intent and the content of the Constitution so that liberal presidents and Congresses might build a welfare state. To get away with this, the Court has invoked the so-called "broad interpretation" of the Constitution— the liberal's way of saying that the law of the land means what they want it to mean. Liberals argue that the Constitution is a "living" document which must be reinterpreted in the light of contemporary conditions. I cannot agree with this. The Constitution is what the founding fathers intended it to be and said it was—not what anyone else says it is. If you subscribe to government by law, you have to accept the Constitution as it was written, and replace outdated portions in accordance with the procedures prescribed by the Constitution. "Any other course," Goldwater has said, "enthrones tyrants and dooms freedom."

In short, by disregarding the principle of states' rights and undermining the authority of the Constitution, liberals have destroyed our primary means of preserving limited government. This is why I find it so difficult to accept your assurances that we can maintain a middle road short of absolute state control or socialism. When men's good intentions are substituted for law, the days of a democracy are numbered.

LIBERAL: The federal government has increasingly assumed certain responsibilities formerly exercised exclusively by the states. But I do not agree with your analysis of the causes and consequences of this expansion of federal power. Liberals are committed just as firmly as conservatives to the principle of states' rights and the constitutional ideal of government by laws; where we disagree is over the correct interpretation and application of the Constitution. Let's begin with a brief look at the liberal view of that crucial document.

At its best, a constitution contains the settled wisdom of a people concerning the proper aims and methods of government. It can't be more, since nothing conceived at a given moment in time can be expected to anticipate every future problem and contingency.

The men who assembled in Philadelphia in the spring of 1787 to create a constitution were surely aware of this limitation on their efforts. The final product of their labor was brief and intentionally general, even vague in parts. For example, the federal government was empowered to collect taxes to provide for the nation's "general Welfare," and to "regulate commerce with foreign Nations, and among the several States." Broad designations like these gave the Constitution the flexibility needed to keep it pertinent in a changing world. Between the powers expressly or implicitly granted to the federal government and those reserved to the states is an area of possible government action in which the lines defining federal power, state power, and concurrent power were only dimly etched. If the Constitution had been more specific in its enumeration and delegation of powers, it would quickly have become unworkable.

As liberals see it, the Constitution is like the blueprint of a house. The blueprint defines the structure and dimensions of the building and sets certain limits on the activity of the builder; it ensures that the final result will be a bungalow and not an apartment building. At the same time, the blueprint permits the builder the freedom to alter the house's exterior as conditions and tastes change—but always within the limits established by the architect's plan. If the builder ignores the framework of the house and the points of greatest stress and strain, an additional room or new construction technique may cause the entire building to collapse.

The Constitution functions in a similar way. It states the kind of government it is seeking to establish—a federal republic—and the ends it wishes that government to serve. Limits are placed on the activities of federal and state governments to keep their performances consistent with those ends. Certain duties and procedures are prescribed to provide a basic framework for organization and operation. But plenty of leeway is left for succeeding generations to build around that framework, as the realities and demands of each age dictate. So, when Congress or the Supreme Court weighs the constitutionality of a proposed or accomplished government action, they hold it up against the broad purposes and methods of government expressed in the Constitution.

This is no simple, cut-and-dried task. In a particular instance, free speech may conflict with the directive to "provide for the common defense." The Supreme Court must decide which ought to be given priority. As I pointed out, many parts of the Constitution are vaguely worded. For example, the federal government is empowered to regulate interstate commerce. Does this mean Washington has the right to impose certain controls on the airline industry? Obviously, the founding fathers didn't have this in mind in 1787. If we were to amend the Constitution every time the president or Congress proposed an action not specifically mentioned, the government would be paralyzed and constitutionalism impossible. So the Supreme Court very properly decides whether the particular controls in question are compatible with the Constitution's aims. This is what we mean by a "broad interpretation" of the Constitution—the evaluation of that document in the light of contemporary conditions.

CONSERVATIVE: Which is another way of saying government by men instead of by laws. Liberals endow nine men with the power to dictate what is constitutional and what isn't, and then they sanctify their decisions as the "law of the land."

LIBERAL: Not so. In the first place, it was the Constitution (Article III, section 2), not New Deal liberals, that gave the Court the power of judicial review. Furthermore, the justices' decisions are circumscribed by the provisions of the Constitution. If the Court were to ignore the general structure and objectives described in the Constitution, the republic might indeed collapse— except that either Congress or the state legislatures can amend the Constitution specifically to alter or reverse the Court's judgment. So men do interpret the meaning of the Constitution, but only within the limits established by law and with the safeguard that the governed can overrule any interpretations they deem unconstitutional. Our public officials must abide by the law; this is scarcely arbitrary rule by men.   *1 0 9 5 9 4*

According to Professor Harry Girvetz in his book *The Evolution of American Liberalism:*

> . . . the constitutional ideal must be spelled out not to prevent the *use* but to prevent the *misuse* or *abuse* of power. A constitution must provide for an efficient organization of the use of power and for founding such use upon popular consent.

I think most liberals would accept this view of the Constitution. As you can see, it complements our belief in the need for a "positive" government that works actively—within specified limits— to help the governed realize the full benefits of liberty.

Having said this, our differences over states' rights ought to be more comprehensible. Liberals certainly subscribe to the dictum that "where any function can be equally well discharged by a central or by a local body, it ought by preference to be entrusted to the local body." But where the local governments can't perform the function as well, or at all, liberals believe the central government should act, *providing* such action is compatible with the aims and methods cited by the Constitution. A city may possess a very poor fire department, but there is nothing the federal government can do about it. This sort of activity is clearly within the jurisdiction of local government. But in areas which are designated to the federal government, or in which the Constitution implies concurrent federal-state powers, Washington has not only the right but the responsibility to move if the need arises.

CONSERVATIVE: How about the 1954 Supreme Court decision to desegregate schools? Is control over education one of these so-called "concurrent" powers?

LIBERAL: I'm no constitutional lawyer, so I can't give you a technical explanation of the Court's reasons for acting. And, of course, even the experts disagree on the proper meaning of the Constitution. But as I understand it, the Court didn't claim any control over the field of education, as such. It based its authority to declare segregated schools unconstitutional on the Fourteenth Amendment, which forbids the states to "deny to any person within [their] jurisdiction the equal protection of the laws." In the case of *Plessy v. Ferguson* in 1896, the Court had ruled that "separate but equal" facilities for whites and Negroes were acceptable under the Constitution's "equal protection" clause. What the justices concluded in 1954 was that separate facilities can never be equal, that they leave the Negro with a damaging sense of inferiority.

It's beside the point whether or not the authors of the Fourteenth Amendment intended it to be applied to education. Do segregated schools deprive Negroes of the equal protection of the laws of the states? Is segregated education consistent with the goals set forth in the Constitution? These were the relevant questions. In spite of the diverse make-up of the Court, which contained both liberals and conservatives, the justices were unanimous in the 1954 decision to outlaw racially segregated schooling.

CONSERVATIVE: But what business is it of those of us who support integration to foist our views on the people of Mississippi? They understand the situation down there better than we do.

LIBERAL: While ours is a federal system, every state in the union is part of the nation—more so than ever before. Today, what the people in Mississippi do vitally affects the people of Minnesota and Maine. When Negroes in certain states receive an inferior education, the whole country suffers. When prejudice and not ability determines what kind of job a man gets, the entire economy is weakened. Federalism and nationalism are not mutually exclusive. To build the kind of society the Constitution envisions, they must be harmonized. Pluralism must be maintained, but not at the expense of unity. This was a further reason why the Supreme Court felt compelled to act in 1954.

There are many other reasons why the federal government has increased its participation in affairs that traditionally rested solely with the states. Needed programs and projects are often too large and too expensive for a state to undertake alone. For instance, a social-insurance system is far more costly to run on a state basis than it is to run nationally; also, the movement of workers from state to state would create impossible administrative problems and potential serious injustices. Large-scale conservation and highway projects are often beyond the immediate means of a particular state government.

CONSERVATIVE: Just a minute. The funds the federal government uses to finance these projects don't appear out of thin air. They are obtained by taxing the citizens of the states. To say the states can't afford something but Washington can is a lot of nonsense. If the federal government didn't tax the American people so heavily, the states could easily raise their taxes enough to meet the needs of their residents.

LIBERAL: You're overlooking two important points. First, most of the wealth in this country is concentrated in a few rich, industrial areas. The states in these areas would have no difficulty providing for their citizens if we followed your advice. But what about the large portions of the nation that aren't so fortunate? A state like West Virginia, with its heavy unemployment and scarce industry, would be in desperate straits. By financing the most costly programs federally, the benefits of our affluence are spread out equitably across the country. Second, industry will often migrate to states where corporation taxes are lowest. State legislators are understandably hesitant to respond to the need for more and better state services for fear of driving out business and increasing unemployment. The federal government can levy taxes and circumvent this problem. One of the purposes of the grant-in-aid programs you criticized is to channel this money back into the states. These programs are then administered in a decentralized fashion by officials who are closest to local problems.

Another cause of increased federal intervention has been the inability or unwillingness of most rurally-dominated state legislatures to face up to the problems of an urban, industrial nation. By clinging to archaic districting arrangements, men representing a minority of a state's population have been able to maintain control of one and sometimes both houses of a legislature. As a result, the cities have found themselves with nowhere to turn but Washington for help in solving their growing difficulties. Hopefully, the Supreme Court's recent "one man, one vote" decision will rectify this unfortunate situation.

Finally, I would like to put your statements about "the dramatic shift of power from the state and local governments to Washington over the past third of a century" into proper perspective. In pointing out the increased role of the federal government, you give the impression that most of the increase has come at the expense of state and local government activity. The fact is that, while government on all levels has expanded considerably, state and local governments have been growing at a much faster rate than the federal government. Between 1955 and 1965, federal employment increased five percent, while state and local governments increased employment by about fifty percent, so great were the demands confronting them. Since World War II, the federal debt has grown roughly twenty-five percent, the debt of state and local governments, almost 600 percent. Furthermore, you failed to note that the 2800 percent increase in defense spending since 1930, in *real* money terms, has been by far the major factor in the upswing in federal expenditures. In short, Washington's increased activity has not been a federal takeover of the country, but a sign of the urgent need for more government services at all levels in our highly urbanized, industrialized society.

I believe the liberal approach to states' rights and the Constitution has succeeded very well in preserving limited government in this country. When a narrow view of these same institutions is allowed to obstruct responsible government action, then people become disillusioned with constitutionalism and turn to government by men. Liberalism has put America not on the "road to serfdom," but on the road to freedom. I see no reason why we should change that course.

4
Accomplishments
of liberal government

The most obvious way to judge a political philosophy or approach is to evaluate how it has performed. Has liberalism accomplished what it set out to do? Has it worked or hasn't it? According to conservatives, liberal government has been a lot of talk and very little effective action. If the conservative is right, liberals are standing on the wrong side of the fence.

There's nothing too complex about responding to this line of conservative attack; it just takes a reasonably broad knowledge of the facts. Economic growth rates, business profits, farm production, and government monetary and fiscal techniques aren't merely abstract principles. They can be translated into dollars, physical quantities, and percentages. However, these results can't be measured meaningfully in a void; they have to be viewed in their proper contexts. Per-capita disposable income in 1937 might not seem impressive unless it is held up against the 1933 level. The old cliché that "it's all relative" will be especially important in this part of the dialogue.

• *The New Deal was a complete failure. If it hadn't been for World War II, people would still be standing in bread lines.*

CONSERVATIVE: It just dawned on me that we've been conducting this discussion backwards. If a dealer shows me a used car which doesn't work and looks as if it never will, I don't stand around debating the cost, the condition of the tires, and where I'm going to drive it. During the last few hours we've been arguing about liberalism's compatibility with individual freedom, its effect on character and initiative, and its transformation of the United States into a socialist state. These are interesting issues, but quite beside the point. American liberalism is such a used car. It hasn't worked since it was put on the market in 1933, and it shows little promise of doing so in the future. If I had brought this out at the start, we would never have gotten involved in this heated dialogue.

The facts speak for themselves. When the Depression struck —a temporary adjustment of the economy which would have worked itself out if left alone—people mistakenly lost faith in our capitalist system and frantically looked about for a savior. Their attention was captured by that eloquent New Yorker, Franklin Delano Roosevelt. Promising the nation a bundle of liberal panaceas which he labeled a "New Deal," he was elected president of the United States.

At long last, liberals had the chance to put their political philosophy to the test. There was a flurry of activity in Washington. The lights in the White House burned late, and during those historic "first hundred days," bill after bill was rushed through Congress to the president's desk. Professors flocked to the Capitol with original schemes to get the economy moving. The government experimented with handouts, public works, make-work, pump priming, youth camps, business codes of conduct, and traveling federal art shows. Motion was the watchword of the New Dealers—motion and more motion.

And when the last of the major Roosevelt proposals became law and the dust settled, people looked around to see where all the motion had taken them. The answer was, nowhere! In 1938, more than ten million men and women were without jobs (twenty percent of the labor force) and the steel industry was producing at the pathetic rate of nineteen percent of capacity. The constant activity had created the illusion of progress, but we were still in the middle of the Depression. Mind you, there were some "achievements": the national debt had swelled from seventeen billion dollars to forty-two billion dollars, the size and cost of government had skyrocketed, federal intervention had become the rule, and the big city bosses and labor leaders had unprecedented power. These were the results of the loudly heralded liberal experiment; this was what the New Deal gave the country.

Ironically, liberals were saved by Hitler and his Nazi legions. Before the full impact of the liberal failure could make itself evident to the American people, we were in a war which demanded national unity and the cessation of political criticism. Production boomed. Prosperity followed. But it was World War II that put us on the road to recovery, not hare-brained liberal planning!

Liberals are quick to produce statistics showing the great advances we have made over the past third of a century. These are misleading, because steady inflation has reduced the dollar to less than half its 1929 purchasing power. Of course our standard of living has improved considerably since the 1920's—that's only to be expected in a nation with an abundance of natural resources, a highly skilled population, and an enterprising business community. Since 1945, pent-up consumer demand and then the outbreak of the cold war have sustained our economic growth. The real question is: How much further ahead would we be if we hadn't been hampered by a meddling government in Washington. Americans should be doubly proud of their progress in recent years, because it has been accomplished in spite of the government, not because of it.

I often hear people say that it is unfair to judge liberalism strictly on its economic performance, that the elimination of social problems is a major liberal objective. Liberal Congresses may have authorized billions of dollars to fight unemployment, poverty, juvenile delinquency, and crime, but are these problems any less with us today than they ever were? In many instances, they have become more acute. It's just another case of liberal motion with no real movement. Anyone who takes the time to study the history of the last three decades can come up with only one conclusion: American liberalism has not succeeded. And when one brand of automobile consistently fails to get you where you want to go, it is time to change to a new make.

LIBERAL: Your analysis of the New Deal is somewhat misleading and it doesn't go far enough. To start with, you make it sound as though the economy hit bottom in 1933 and stayed there until the outbreak of the war. One look at the usual economic indicators shows this was not the case. By the end of 1933, the country's gross national product had fallen to 153 billion dollars (1964 dollars), thirty percent below its 1929 level of 217.8 billion dollars (1964 dollars). In 1937, after four years of New Deal "meddling," our GNP climbed above its precrash peak to 219.5 billion dollars (1964 dollars). Per capita disposable income (the average income each American had to spend *after* taxes) showed a similar pattern. Falling from $1,273 in 1929 to $938 in 1933 (all in 1964 dollars), it was back up to $1,254 by 1939. By most measures, liberal government had reversed the direction of the economy during the thirties and nursed it back to its 1929 condition.

However, as you pointed out, the problem of mass unemployment lingered—24.9 percent of the labor force had been without jobs in 1933 and 17.2 percent were still unemployed in 1939—and a healthy growth rate had not materialized. It took the war to put everyone back to work and to get the economy moving at a prosperous pace. Strange as it may seem, this proved that the

New Dealers had hit upon the right techniques for stimulating our sluggish economy. Let me elaborate.

When FDR entered the White House, he had no set plan for ending the Depression and no dogmatic notions of what had to be done. He had promised the American people that their welfare was the government's cardinal concern, and that he and the Congress would do everything in their power to lead the country out of the gloom.

Then, as you mentioned, the experimentation began. There was no comprehensive blueprint; government measures were often contradictory, like Congress' decision in 1936 to reduce taxes and cut government expenditures—the latter nullifying the intended effect of the former upon the economy. Some of the President's advisors urged him not to abandon orthodox means for dealing with economic crises, such as balancing the budget and using self-restraint to allow the disequilibrium of the economy to right itself in a free market. Others sought to sell him on Lord Keynes' thesis that the economy lacked a demand for goods and services which could only be provided through massive government spending and a budgetary deficit. Roosevelt was caught in between, and his inability to choose decisively one approach or the other meant that neither was given a fair chance to show what it could do.

It was the Japanese bombardment of Pearl Harbor and our involvement in World War II that put Keynes' suggestions into practice. The war effort, in an economic sense, can be likened to a gigantic public works project. Government demand for goods and services to prosecute the war led many industries to increase production. Laid-off employees were called back to work and the wages they received created new demand for consumer items. Perceiving the growing ability of the public to buy things, businessmen invested in additional plants and equipment, which created more jobs, more demand, and more investment. Within a couple of years, demand rose to the full employment level, and the problem became too much money competing for a limited supply of output—the problem of climbing prices or inflation.

The New Dealers had tried public works programs and tax cuts which should have had the same successful effects. But, unsure of these untested economic tools, they failed to employ them on a large enough scale. It remained for the Kennedy and Johnson administrations to show that these tools could be effective in peacetime as well as in war.

Does this mean, then, that liberal government during the thirties was just an enormously expensive laboratory in which new techniques for stimulating the economy were tested? To view the New Deal in this light is to miss its greatest impact. All of that "motion and more motion" in Washington, plus Roosevelt's ability to convince the majority of people that the government would stand by them through those desperate days, combined to restore America's confidence in democratic government and in an essentially capitalist economy. Both the extreme right and the extreme left in this country were showing signs of strength and possible mass support. Fascist and Communist demagogues were demanding "share the wealth" schemes or were calling for the violent overthrow of the government. But the concern Washington showed for the individual's problems stole their thunder. As the perennial Socialist candidate for president, Norman Thomas, remarked, it was FDR who killed socialism in the United States.

The groups with the best reasons for being dissatisfied during the Depression—the unemployed, the unskilled workers, the Negroes, and the members of ethnic and religious minorities—were given a voice in national affairs which they previously had been denied. Presidential encouragement and legislation such as the Wagner Act made labor's theoretical right to organize a reality. A Civil Rights division was established in the Justice Department. Roman Catholics, Jews, and citizens of southern and eastern European parentage found they were being judged in Washington on the basis of their abilities alone. Roosevelt saw to it that those with the least to lose in the event of radical change gained a stake in the existing order. By contrast, Britain's Conservative government failed to demonstrate a willingness to act and a compassion for those who were hit hardest by the Depression, and at the end of the war saw itself turned out in favor of Clement Attlee's Socialist government. I don't think it is any exaggeration to say that liberalism rescued democracy and capitalism in America at a time when they no longer appeared able to meet the people's needs. *This* was the profound significance of the New Deal.

Now let's look at liberalism's performance over the full thirty-three-year period. You commented that a lot of growth statistics are misleading because inflation has halved the value of the dollar. Here are some figures in 1964 dollars which are adjusted for inflation; that is, dollars expressed in terms of the same purchasing power, so we can measure real changes instead of money changes. In 1929—we'll use this prosperity year rather than 1933, which was the bottom of the Depression—the total value of the goods and services produced in this country (our gross national product) was 217.8 billion dollars in terms of 1964. By 1964, our GNP had increased 185 percent to 622.3 billion dollars. Per-capita disposable income jumped from $1,273 to $2,248 over the same period. Remember, this is real change. Total financial savings by individuals grew from 10.5 billion dollars in 1939 (the earliest year for which figures are available) to 27.9 billion dollars in 1964. Average hourly earnings in real purchasing power more than doubled from $1.18 just before the Crash to $2.54 in 1964. And corporate profits *after* taxes climbed steadily from 17.4 billion dollars in 1929 to 31.6 billion dollars in 1964, all in 1964 dollars. This is not illusory progress. America has grown tremendously under liberal leadership!

In discussing this expansion, you raised an interesting question: How can liberals be so sure that this economic growth is a result of their policies and planning and not just the normal performance of an enterprising people in a richly endowed nation? The answer, quite frankly, is that there is no way to measure the exact effects on the economy of monetary and fiscal policies. But the evidence of a causal relationship is overwhelming.

For example, as succeeding presidents and Congresses have become more confident and skilled in the use of such economic tools as the Federal Reserve System and the tax rate, and have strengthened the effectiveness of built-in stabilizers like unemployment insurance and the minimum wage, the length and severity of the recessions that have plagued America since the mid-nineteenth century have greatly diminished. During the slump that followed World War I, industrial output fell by thirty-two percent, personal income by twenty-two percent, and retail sales by four percent. Compare this with the recession after World War II, in which industrial output dropped by only nine percent, personal income by four percent, and retail sales by an insignificant 0.3 percent.

An even better indication of the value of the new liberal economics can be seen by contrasting the economy's performance during the Eisenhower years with its behavior under the Kennedy and Johnson administrations. In the 1950's no attempt was made to utilize most of the methods of economic management that had been acquired during the crisis-ridden thirties and forties. "Times are normal again," went the reasoning. "There's no need to manipulate, guide, and adjust—the free-market forces will insure adequate expansion." The result was a sluggish economy with an anemic average annual growth rate of 2.5 percent.

John F. Kennedy was the first American president to apply the new economics in a comprehensive, coordinated fashion. Following Congress' directive in the Employment Act of 1946 that it be "the continuing policy and responsibility of the Federal Government to use all practicable means . . . to promote maximum employment, production, and purchasing power," he laid his plans for accelerated growth. Though he didn't live to see their full effect, he would have been proud of the results. To date, we have enjoyed nearly sixty consecutive months of rising prosperity—a national peacetime record—with no end in sight, and an average annual growth rate during the Kennedy-Johnson years of five percent (in *real* money terms). You can still argue that we would have done as well or better if the government had left the economy alone, but the burden of proof is on you to explain how. We now have a history of proven performance behind us. It's possible we might have recovered faster from the Depression without liberal intervention—though I don't see how —but, by the same token, there might have been no Depression at all if present liberal techniques had been understood and implemented in the years before the Crash.

Even this is far from the complete record of progress under liberalism. Many of the improvements in individual and national well-being since 1933 don't lend themselves to statistical summary. Remember the bank runs that were so common even during the prosperous twenties? An average of 634 banks a year failed between 1921 and 1929, destroying the hopes and security of hundreds of thousands of American families. These failures are virtually nonexistent today. Primary credit for this accomplishment must go to one of the products of Roosevelt's "first hundred days," the Federal Deposit Insurance Corporation, which insures individual depositors against losses up to $10,000.

When our fathers used to dabble in stocks before they lost their shirts in the Crash of '29, they had no way of obtaining adequate information on issues old or new—those were the days when stocks were watered more than gardens—and no assurance that the information they did receive was honest and accurate. This state of buyer ignorance coupled with the big bull market margins of ten to fifteen percent had a great deal to do with the wild speculation that preceded the market's collapse. Today, thanks to the Securities Act of 1933 and the Securities Exchange Act of 1934, we are protected against the deceptive manipulation of stocks and are guaranteed full information on securities we contemplate buying or selling. In addition, the Securities and Exchange Commission requires investors currently to pay about seventy percent cash for their purchases, one of a number of measures to prevent another Wall Street debacle.

Before the New Deal, less than half (45.5 percent) of the

factory workers in the United States enjoyed an eight-hour day. Fifty-one-hour and fifty-four-hour weeks were common, with some men being forced to put in fifty-seven and sixty hours a week to hold a job. The eight-hour day, forty-hour week with time-and-a-half for overtime didn't suddenly fall from heaven; it was the result of the Walsh-Healy Act of 1936 and the Fair Labor Standards Act of 1938. The same holds true for the minimum wage of $1.25 an hour, unemployment and disability insurance, and on-the-job health and safety regulations. They were the fruit of federal actions to increase the security and standard of living of the American working man.

The life of the typical farmer in this country used to be characterized by almost total geographic and intellectual isolation and grueling days of the most difficult physical labor. This may have seemed idyllic to the poets who helped spin the agrarian myth, but the ever-increasing number of farmers' sons and daughters who abandoned the countryside for the city was eloquent testimony to the dullness and drudgery of rural living. More than anything else, the establishment of the Rural Electrification Administration in 1934 changed much of this. When FDR became president, only eleven percent of the nation's rural homes could afford the "luxury" of electricity; today nearly ninety-eight percent have it. This means telephones, radios, televisions, and a thousand and one labor-saving machines and appliances for the farmer and his wife. The REA was a federal creation that literally revolutionized America's farm lands.

I've only scratched the surface. I could give you examples of liberal legislation and programs which have increased our security and incomes, improved our health, education, and technology, and expanded business opportunities, labor's ability to organize, and the civil liberties of every citizen. America is unquestionably a better place today than it was three decades ago; and much of this change for the good is a direct result of the principles and practice of liberal government. Liberals don't base their claims to future national leadership on the possession of a crystal ball or of any magical economic potions; they base them on a third of a century of moving the country forward and improving the lot of the individual American. I can't think of a more relevant recommendation.

• *Liberals fail to understand the laws of supply and demand. Their fiscal manipulations have served only to upset the functioning of the free market.*

CONSERVATIVE: This monetary and fiscal manipulation that liberals rely on may produce some short-run gains, but in the long run it only serves to upset the natural balance of the economy. The laws of supply and demand are descriptions of reality which are no more subject to man's meddling than Newton's laws of motion. Besides, no one who has any knowledge of Western history would want to interfere with the workings of the free market.

Whenever enterprise has been left to its own devices, efficient development and prosperity have been the result. How do you think these United States grew from thirteen struggling colonies to the wealthiest nation in the history of the world? It certainly wasn't by interfering with interest rates and telling businessmen what wages to pay. Before the liberals took over Washington, the government knew that progress is achieved by forcing individuals to depend on their own initiative and industry. In an unfettered economy the problems of unemployment, inflation, and recession—which liberals have dreamed up so many unsuccessful schemes and squandered so much money to cure—are justly and effectively eliminated by the forces of supply and demand. You seem unwilling to accept the experience of the past if it doesn't accord with your preconceived plans, no matter what the cost to the country.

The federal government today reminds me of a grotesque juggler who adds another arm every time there is a new ball to keep

in the air. To make the show impressive and the audience atten-
tive, he keeps adding more and more arms until he becomes
hopelessly ensnared and confused, and drops everything. To
maintain the economy's performance, liberal government planners devise new controls and regulations, each of which requires
an additional administrative agency or commission. When these
innovations introduce problems of their own, they add new interventions and new federal bodies. It is only a matter of time
before the entire artificial contraption will come crashing down
upon us, making the Crash of '29 look insignificant in comparison.

LIBERAL: Now you've brought three new charges into our discussion. To start with, you accuse liberals of "meddling" with
the laws of supply and demand. I am not at all sure what you
mean by this. Supply and demand interact in one way in the
Soviet Union, in another way in Great Britain, and in still a
different way in the United States. For that matter, the factors
influencing supply and demand in the American economy today
differ from those that were operative in 1945, 1900, 1820, and
1685. To speak simply of *the* law of supply and demand without
specifying time and place doesn't make much sense.

But assuming, for the moment, that we can agree on a description of the market forces relevant to our own mid-twentieth
century economy, I still do not understand your equation of
government intervention with "meddling." Physicists studied the
phenomenon of friction not to acquire a greater sense of awe,
but to learn how to overcome its destructive qualities in mechanisms with moving parts. The results of their efforts were ball
bearings and axle grease, not a hands-off reverence. The same
holds true for the economy. Economists investigate the business
cycle out of intellectual curiosity and in the hope of finding a
way to eliminate these damaging swings. In some instances their
findings may suggest a noninterference policy, in which case the
action prescribed is no action. This is quite different from con-

cluding that understanding something logically entails the complete acceptance of a situation as it is, which is what you implied.

CONSERVATIVE: You understood what I meant. From the founding of this nation in 1783 until 1933, economic decisions such as the determination of prices, wages, employment, and output were left to the free operation of the market. Of course, economic conditions were in constant flux over this period and the interaction of supply and demand was influenced by ever-changing factors. I am willing to concede all of this. My point is that the economy always managed to adjust to change without government interference, and to achieve tremendous expansion and prosperity. In short, we had an approach to the national economy which was unmatched for success anywhere in the world.

LIBERAL: This brings us to your second charge: that liberals abandoned a way of dealing with the economy which had worked well for 150 years. When you say this, you give the impression that the federal government dutifully kept its finger out of the economy until March 4, 1933, at which date it suddenly had its hands in everything. History just does not back you up in this.

Long before the New Deal, the federal government played a crucial role in the growth and development of the country. The vast unsettled tracts of land beyond the Appalachians were federally managed. Federal money helped build the canals of the 1820's and 1830's that linked inland producers with coastal markets. Cheap land in the West was made available to almost anyone who wanted it by the Homestead Act of 1861; and frontier settlers were protected from hostile Indians by federal cavalry. The single greatest factor in the expansion of this country during the second half of the nineteenth century, the construction of the transcontinental railroads, was made possible by heavy federal subsidies. Federal tariffs protected our infant industries and gave American businessmen an advantage at home against foreign competition. The Sherman Antitrust Act, passed by Congress in 1890, forbade commercial combinations and monopolies in restraint of interstate trade—the list stretches on and on. These are a few of the numerous instances of government economic intervention that occurred before anyone had even heard of Franklin Delano Roosevelt.

There is no denying that federal intervention did increase considerably when liberals went to Washington in 1933. Despite what you've said, the economy's performance over the years left much to be desired. After the Civil War, periods of prosperity were more and more often followed by severe economic setbacks. There were terrible depressions in 1873, 1893, and 1921 and then the general collapse beginning in 1929. With each successive depression the recovery period was longer and human suffering more acute. It was no longer a matter of a few people out of work for several weeks or months. When FDR took the presidential oath, the country was in the grip of an economic decline which, after four years, still was showing no signs of an upswing. Twelve million men and women—twenty-five percent of the labor force—were unemployed, and some had been without jobs and income for the entire four years.

The Great Depression pushed people beyond the limits of acquiescence. Men who had been preaching for years that serious shortcomings had developed in the operation of the free market in this country suddenly acquired the support of the millions of industrious, hard-working Americans who found themselves out of work and out of money through no fault of their own. Any expression of the old idea that the unfettered forces of supply and demand would reward initiative and punish sloth sounded like a cruel joke to those who lived in the Hoovervilles and waited in the bread lines.

This shift of sentiment that swept America failed to move many conservatives, who clung more tenaciously than ever to the accepted economic doctrine of government noninterference or laissez faire. But the growing public demand for action from

Washington was not the mistaken cry of a panicked people, as so many conservatives supposed; it reflected real changes in the economy that had been taking place for over a century.

State laissez faire had been originally suggested by the classical school of English economists in the late eighteenth century and early nineteenth century. Confronted by a British economy in the first stages of the industrial revolution, they reasoned that a country characterized by many small producers and conditions of near-perfect competition could best realize growth and freedom by allowing the economy to work without government intervention. This radical departure from the prevailing mercantilist philosophy, which favored strict state management of the economy, was justified by pointing to the emergence of new realities.

Under the influence of the new economics, American leaders met with little difficulty in applying this policy to their young, undeveloped country. Although the government in Washington did work to promote growth and expansion, it had no need to concern itself with prices, wages, employment, and anticompetitive practices. The United States in the early decades of the nineteenth century was an agrarian nation whose limited industry consisted of small family firms. No single buyer or seller was powerful enough to affect the market, so that the determination of prices and wages rested with the forces of free competition. If an industry folded, a man could find a job in another industry with no difficulty, because extensive division of labor and specialization were still to come in the future. Wages were relatively high, owing to the scarcity of manpower in the New World, and if an individual didn't think he was receiving his worth, he could go into business for himself or buy a few hundred acres of government land and start farming. Whatever the strengths and weaknesses of the limited laissez-faire policy employed in early America, it apparently worked to the satisfaction of the majority of people.

However, as time passed and the United States became progressively industrialized, fundamental changes in the economy

occurred. In the years following the Civil War, competition became far from perfect in many industries. In the oil and steel
industries, for example, a few giant corporations cornered the
market and killed what competition remained by means of price
setting and market-pooling agreements. Industrial growth had
forced labor to specialize, which meant that a man trained to
work in the blast furnaces of Pittsburgh might not be able to
land a job doing something else if fired or laid off. Consumers
and workers were at the mercy of corporations and trusts which
could dictate prices and wages. As the torrent of immigrants
from southern and eastern Europe poured into the country, labor grew plentiful, wages plummeted, and "unemployment" was
added to the economy's vocabulary.

Bigness and interdependence meant that the failure of one
holding company or banking house could send the whole economy reeling. International cartels tied our economy closely to
events in Europe and elsewhere. The economy began to perform
erratically. Forces had come to control it which were beyond the
reach of the average American; as an individual, he was helpless
to shape his own fate. In short, the economic realities that had
made laissez faire a workable government policy had passed.
Growth and freedom were still the national goals, but government nonintervention was no longer a means of obtaining them.

The Great Depression brought this fact home to millions of
Americans with lasting impact. Conservative insistence that the
economy would restore itself if only the government would be
patient and not interfere did not mollify the ruined and jobless;
they didn't want a return to the old order with its insecurity and
threat of future mass unemployment, wiped-out savings, human
degradation, and suffering. Conservatives still refused to recognize the new economic facts of life and the attitudes they engendered. It was left to liberals to grasp these realities and to accept
the challenge of finding new solutions to unprecedented social
and economic problems.

In essence, the New Deal was a pledge by the federal government that the America which emerged from the Depression

would not be identical to the America that had preceded it. Economic growth and freedom would still be objectives, but they must be supplemented with security, increased economic opportunity, greater rights for labor, a larger voice in national affairs for religious, racial, and ethnic minorities, and enough rational management of the economy to provide stability and prevent the recurrence of 1929. Monetary and fiscal policy became part of a new economics which was justified by liberals in much the same way that their classical predecessors had explained their economic "heresies"—by pointing to new realities.

As I tried to demonstrate earlier, these liberal techniques for guiding the economy have worked well. This still leaves unanswered your third charge that, in the long run, these liberal manipulations will destroy the "natural balance" of the economy and result in economic collapse. At what point short-run successes can be considered long run, I'm not sure. A third of a century does not strike me as terribly short run. I already pointed out the declining severity and lengths of the recessions that have occurred since 1933 and the impressive growth rates achieved by the Kennedy and Johnson administrations. I don't know what else I can do to convince you. There is certainly no black magic or hocus-pocus involved in measures like unemployment insurance or the recent tax cut.

• *Deficit spending and a growing national debt are bankrupting the country.*

CONSERVATIVE: There is one aspect of liberal performance that you have assiduously avoided so far: a third of a century of deficit spending and the resulting national debt. As a businessman, I know that deficit spending over a period of time is bound to lead to bankruptcy. You simply cannot spend more money than you take in and expect not to take the consequences. Yet, this is exactly what you liberals are trying to do.

In 1932, the last year of conservative government in Washington, the federal debt totaled 20.8 billion dollars. Today it is more than 320 billion dollars—equal to one-half our entire gross national product! With every increase in the debt, you increase the burden on future generations who will have to pay it off to avoid economic collapse. An economy cannot be built and sustained on a foundation of paper promises.

I'm aware that much of the debt was accumulated fighting World War II, and perhaps there was no alternative at the time. But instead of planning surpluses after the war to retire the debt, liberals kept running up new deficits and adding to the amount the government owes. You may call this "fiscal responsibility" —we don't.

You claim that liberals are doing nothing to upset the balance of the economy. What about deficit spending? Prosperity is purchased for today with no regard for the bill that will have to be paid tomorrow. The government already spends eleven billion dollars a year just to meet the interest on the debt; imagine the financial chaos when it comes time to retire the principal.

Liberalism may have produced some results since 1933, but if deficits and debt were essential to those results, the cost of national progress was far too high.

LIBERAL: I think I can satisfactorily defend the debt and deficit spending, but it will take a little time.

CONSERVATIVE: Go right ahead. If you can show me how I can spend more than I earn and get away with it, I'll gladly listen.

LIBERAL: To start with, it is important to realize that deficit spending is not limited to government. Every year millions of consumers purchase appliances and automobiles on the installment plan, thousands buy houses with mortgages. Businesses commonly borrow funds from banks or issue bonds in order to expand and buy new equipment. In fact, consumer and corporate debt has been growing steadily since World War II, and far from being a sign of financial difficulty, it reflects tremendous national prosperity. The result of all this private borrowing is more houses, vacuum cleaners, factories, and machines. A rising debt total is not just a paper structure; it often represents a growing total of real assets.

Government borrowing works the same way. Much of the money raised through the sale of government bonds goes to create real wealth such as schools, highways, homes, hospitals, research facilities, stockpiles of strategic materials, dams, airports, and harbors. In other words, a large part of the debt is a claim against things which physically exist.

When you discuss the financial condition of your business, you don't talk just about your liabilities; you consider them in relation to your assets. For some reason, when the government's debt is mentioned, no one takes its assets into account. If this were done, there would be a lot less concern about the federal debt.

How the government's real assets are appraised can be the subject of some discussion, but the important thing to note is that there is a considerable amount of assets. Federal expenditures do not, as some enthusiastic opponents claim, represent money "poured down a rat hole." The country has used part of its expenditures to create tangible assets, many of which are revenue-producing. And tangible assets are only a small part of the real assets created by federal expenditures. The bulk of them show up in the earning power of the country and are measured by the gross national product.

CONSERVATIVE: Let's go back to your comparison of government deficit spending and private borrowing. Sure, people buy on the installment plan, but eventually they must pay off their debt or lose their purchases. I do not see the government paying off the national debt.

LIBERAL: Of course, individual debts have to be paid off, but not the total or aggregate private debt. While individual borrowers are continually paying off their debts, other borrowers are incurring new ones, so the *total* private debt will never be paid off. Moreover, sheer population growth can be expected to cause aggregate private debt to grow steadily.

With business borrowing, it's common for a single firm *never* to pay off its outstanding debt. Look at the American Telephone and Telegraph Company, for example. In 1929, AT&T carried a total debt of 1.2 billion dollars; in 1962, that debt was more than 8.4 billion dollars. This expansion was accomplished by what is known as bond refunding. When AT&T's old bonds fell due, it would issue new bonds to repay the old ones. As long as AT&T's earning power remains high enough to pay the interest on the bonds, and as long as the bond-buying public retains enough confidence in AT&T's continued success to keep buying new bond issues, there is no problem. Do you find investors worrying about AT&T's financial position because it carries an 8.4 billion dollar debt that will probably get bigger in the years ahead? Quite the reverse: AT&T stock is considered a "blue chip of the blue chips." Because people have faith in the company's future earning power, they have confidence in the bonds it issues and in its ability to meet its obligations.

The federal government operates in the same way. It has to meet its obligations, but it does not have to pay off the national debt. Each year, millions of dollars worth of bonds are bought back by the government as they mature. These bonds are repaid exactly as AT&T repaid its bonded debt—by refunding: selling a new issue to pay for the old. So you see, just as total private debt need never be repaid, our national debt never has to be paid off.

Furthermore, the government is in even a stronger position to finance its debt than business. Government income is certain, short of a total collapse of our society, so its credit rating is the best in the country. Most private firms have to rely on the performance of their products in a competitive market for their incomes; the government has the power to raise money to pay the interest on its bonds by taxing—there is no risk. In addition,

Americans are always willing to buy new government bond issues because the physical assets behind the national debt are worth billions, and because confidence in the continued existence of the government is high.

CONSERVATIVE: If public debt is as much like private debt as you say, there has to be a limit on its size. I can only go into debt so far before I become bankrupt. Isn't a national debt of 320 billion dollars dangerously large?

LIBERAL: To quote absolute figures is meaningless. A $100,-000 debt might bankrupt you or me but it wouldn't seriously affect Paul Getty. One corporation might borrow a million dollars to build a modern plant and go bankrupt because the earnings of the new plant were not large enough to pay the interest and amortization on the debt, while another firm might borrow twice as much with the only result being bigger profits. In short, a person can afford to borrow as much as his income and current expenses allow him to pay in the way of interest and amortization.

The best measure of the country's economic output is the gross national product (GNP) which measures annually all goods and services the country produces. The national debt has a close relation to the GNP. Government policies affect the growth of the economy and hence the GNP; conversely, the size of the GNP measures the country's ability to pay taxes and hence its ability to carry the national debt.

At the end of World War II the national debt was larger than the GNP by twenty-eight percent. A whole year's income of the entire nation was thus less than the debt. Yet nothing drastic happened; remember that mortgage companies are accustomed to lending from two-and-a-half to three times a person's annual income for the purchase of a home. Since World War II, the GNP has increased much more rapidly than the debt, so that today the debt is less than fifty percent of the GNP. The debt wasn't a serious burden in 1946; it is even less of one now.

Seen in relation to the growth of other kinds of debt, the increase in the federal debt in recent years is very small. The national debt has grown only twenty-five percent since 1947, while private debt has risen 420 percent and the debt of state and local governments almost 600 percent. It is clear that the "burden of the debt," when viewed in its proper context, has been decreasing as the country grows and certainly falls within the range of debt that the government can carry with no difficulty or danger to the economy as a whole.

One other point should be made here. Unlike a private corporation, when the federal government invests in a long-term asset —that is to say, when it builds a road, constructs a post office, or buys a computer—the outlay of funds in a particular year is considered an operating expense and not a capital expenditure. In private business a distinction is made between operating expenses and long-term capital investments. The long-term investment is paid for over a period of years. If an outlay is made in a particular year for a piece of machinery or a new building, the asset is depreciated over its lifetime and only the yearly cost is counted as an expenditure. But when the federal government acquires or builds something, the *total* cost is counted as an operating expense in the year of the purchase.

If AT&T, which has the highest capitalization of any company in the United States, were to treat its capital investments as does the federal government, it would operate in the red every year! To put it another way, if the government were to treat its capital investments in the same way as private industry, the federal budget would have shown a huge surplus in every year since 1946.

CONSERVATIVE: But you still haven't told me why future generations should be forced to pay for our extravagance.

LIBERAL: The question is whether we will be leaving future generations an extravagance or a going business. You seem to condemn all government debt, forgetting that we're leaving future generations a very productive economy, and that the strength of the economy is far outrunning the burden of the debt. We might put it this way: At the end of World War II the situation facing future generations was like that of an heir who had inherited a business with an income of $100,000 and a debt of $128,000. The heir has done right well with the business. The generation that inherits the national economy in 1966 will inherit a business with an income of more than $300,000 and a debt of $150,000.

CONSERVATIVE: Maybe the government can meet its obligations —but why not pay off the debt? It costs taxpayers eleven billion dollars a year in interest charges.

LIBERAL: If we don't mind the effect upon the level of the economy and our economic growth, paying off the debt might well be done. It would mean taxing one part of the population and paying off another. We clearly have the taxing capacity to do this if we wish. But the effect on the economy of taking a lot of purchasing power away from the public and giving it to the holders of bonds would disrupt our whole economic system. And what would the ex-bondholders do with the cash? Where can they find a better investment?

CONSERVATIVE: At least we would be freed from that eleven-billion-dollar-a-year interest obligation.

LIBERAL: Those payments are no drain on the nation's wealth because ninety-five percent of the debt is owed to American taxpayers. Only five percent of the interest paid leaves the country.

Look at it this way. When the government sells bonds to finance its buying, it does so instead of charging more taxes. The money which bondholders lend to the government is used to spare the taxpayers from paying more taxes. In a sense, then, the taxpayers have borrowed money from the bond buyers.

Since the people who are lending money to the taxpayers are taxpayers themselves, Americans owe the national debt to Americans. If every taxpayer held bonds, every taxpayer would owe part of the national debt to himself.

CONSERVATIVE: Assuming, for the purposes of argument, that the national debt is not harmful, you still haven't shown me what is to be gained by increasing the government's obligations through the use of planned deficits. Why, for instance, when we had a tax cut recently didn't we reduce government expenditures by the same amount? I don't see how this constant spending of more than we take in can be considered sound economics.

LIBERAL: I mentioned a minute ago that a deficit can be very helpful in stimulating the economy. How does this work? In 1946 the Employment Act made the federal government officially responsible for promoting stable economic growth and full employment. One of the most effective devices used to carry out this directive is the federal budget. Because it can be expanded or contracted—within modest limits—and because taxes can be expanded or contracted—also within appropriate limits—the federal budget can be used to increase or to decrease economic activity. By spending more or taxing less, the federal government gives immediate impetus to economic activity; by spending less or taxing more, the economy can be slowed down. Of course either trend is of short duration, but long enough to have an important effect in expanding or contracting the economy.

At the beginning of 1964 the economy was operating below its potential; five percent of the labor force was out of work and many factories reported unused productive capacity. This time the solution decided upon was a tax cut. Reducing personal income taxes automatically gave consumers a greater share of their income to spend. The new spending caused businesses to increase production and employ more men. Greater profits and larger payrolls meant more money in people's pockets and still more spending. As factories began to operate near capacity, businessmen invested in new plants and equipment, which led to more employment, more investments, and yet greater demand.

If the government had reduced its spending by the amount of the tax cut—which is what you were suggesting—the increased spending by consumers and businesses would have been offset and the aggregate demand would have remained unchanged. All that would have happened is that the burden of unemployment and unused capacity would have shifted from areas in which consumers and businesses bought to those in which the government bought. Instead of unemployment among auto workers, there would have been airplane factory workers looking for jobs. But by cutting taxes and holding federal spending constant, the government was able to accelerate our growth rate and increase employment. And did you know that the tax revenue from the additional income generated by the tax cut actually reduced the year's federal deficit?

Despite what conservatives say, there are no unbalancing effects in any of this. The government's fiscal policy is merely a tool for keeping supply and demand in balance at one level of employment and output rather than another. If you still think there is any black magic involved, take a paper and pencil and the 1963 *Economic Report of the President* and trace through the workings of the tax cut step by step.

CONSERVATIVE: I will do that. But I don't think it will cure my worries.

LIBERAL: Maybe not—and maybe it shouldn't. All of us ought to worry a little about the debt and deficit financing and government spending. But not just blind worry, not just jitters. Let's make our worrying selective and constructive.

• *Private enterprise has been crippled by regulation and harried by government competition.*

CONSERVATIVE: In our discussion so far, you've boasted about liberal legislation to protect consumers and to strengthen labor. This may be all well and good, but you never mentioned the weakening effects these same measures have had on private business—the life-blood of what is left of our free enterprise system. In what even you admit is intended to be an essentially capitalist economy, it's hard to reconcile your claim of national progress under liberalism with the fact that liberal government has stifled business growth through intervention and direct competition.

Earlier you admitted to being in agreement with Barry Goldwater's belief that the individual is the best judge of his own interests. As I'm sure you are aware, the vast majority of businessmen in this country have opposed liberal programs every step of the way since 1933. With each new federal regulation and control they have warned Congress that commerce would suffer. But their protests have been in vain. Washington has persisted in hampering business by dictating methods of production, financing, marketing, and advertising. Instead of creating a balance between labor and business—which would have benefited the country—the government has allowed the union bosses to set wages and production standards. Now this could hardly be expected to promote business growth. Then with schemes like the Tennessee Valley Authority (TVA) and the Rural Electrification Administration (REA) liberals have put the government in direct competition with private enterprise, on terms that insured government success. No wonder so few businessmen are liberals!

I am in favor of giving the consumer and the working man a fair break. But liberals have gone too far. By retarding the growth of free enterprise, you injure everyone; not only businessmen, but, in the long run, consumers and laborers as well. When businesses are prevented from expanding to their full potential and operating at top efficiency, it's not only profits that suffer; prices invariably rise and unemployment increases. Progress in a capitalist country has to bring improved business performance and conditions. For this reason, the liberal cry of progress in America since the New Deal rings hollow in my ears.

LIBERAL: I fully agree with your statement that improvement in business conditions and performance is an essential ingredient of progress. But this does not contradict my contention that America has progressed tremendously under liberal government.

Look at the facts. When conservatives left the White House in the beginning of 1933, free enterprise wasn't exactly booming. To be exact, in 1932—the last year of conservative control in Washington—corporate profits after taxes in 1964 dollars totaled an august 8.8 billion dollars in the red. Most businesses were losing money. Since 1933, aggregate business profits have always been in the black. Even when we use the prosperity year of 1929 as a starting point, business growth under liberal government has been impressive. In the year preceding the Crash, corporate profits after taxes (in 1964 dollars) were 17.4 billion dollars. In 1964 they stood at 31.6 billion dollars—an increase of eighty-two percent in *real* money terms. With the comprehensive implementation of liberal techniques for stimulating economic growth, the increase in profits has been nothing short of spectacular. During the four years of the Kennedy-Johnson administrations, corporate profits after taxes rose steadily from a rate of 19.5 billion dollars early in 1961 to nearly 32 billion dollars at the end of 1964. Judged by any standard, this is progress.

Another measure of performance is the annual failure rate of businesses. In 1929, 104 out of every 10,000 firms closed their doors. By 1964, the fatality rate had fallen to 53 of every 10,000 firms, or approximately one-half the pre-Crash level. Business expenditures on new plants and equipment have more than tripled from the 1939 total (this is the earliest available figure) of 13.5 billion dollars (in 1964 dollars) to 44.66 billion dollars in 1964. You implied that liberal intervention prevented manufacturers from improving their productive efficiency. In the last seventeen years, output per man-hour has increased seventy percent. Quite simply, the figures show that the business sector in the United States has thrived with liberals in the White House and Congress.

And what about the other half of our criterion for measuring business improvement, the conditions under which businessmen must operate? Nothing is more important to the business community than continued economic growth with freedom from violent ups and downs in the business cycle. When an economy lacks stability, businessmen have difficulty planning output, investment, and employment. This uncertainty inhibits business growth, because owners and management hesitate to undertake long-range expansion programs for fear that a serious setback may catch them overextended.

As I described earlier, our liberal monetary and fiscal policies have given the economy a degree of stability that it never had before. Again, let's consult the facts. In the 1920-21 recession following World War I, industrial output dropped thirty-two percent, personal income twenty-two percent, and retail sales fourteen percent. During the Great Depression, between 1929 and 1933, industrial output and personal income both declined a catastrophic fifty-two percent, with retail sales falling forty-four percent. While the recession of 1937-38 represented a serious setback on all fronts, the built-in stabilizers designed by the New Dealers were already beginning to yield results. Though industrial output fell thirty-two percent, personal income was reduced only eleven percent.

But it was after the war that the techniques for stabilization and cycle control started by Roosevelt and developed by his successors revealed their full effects. In the post-war recession of 1948-49, industry's output went down nine percent—only a quarter of the drop recorded in the post-war recession of the twenties—personal income dropped four percent, while retail sales declined a trifling 0.3 percent. The next low period, 1953-54, also registered an industrial drop of nine percent. This time, however, personal income declined only 0.2 percent and retail sales one percent. Finally, in 1957-58, when industrial output dropped fourteen percent, personal income repeated its 1948-49 performance by losing a mere 0.3 percent, with retail sales falling three percent. Since that drop, the nation and the American business community have experienced seven years of uninterrupted prosperity. And, as I pointed out before, the annual growth rate during the Kennedy-Johnson years has been a vigorous five percent in *real* money terms.

Another way that liberals have increased stability has been to push measures to correct weaknesses in the banking system and securities market—weaknesses made obvious by the collapse on Wall Street and the ensuing depression. Also, businessmen are presently offerred many government services to help them locate and develop profitable markets for their products abroad. These services were not available prior to 1933.

Of course, federal regulations do govern certain business practices. Goods which people eat or wear must meet specified health and sanitation standards; certain techniques of marketing and advertising are outlawed by federal statute; and commercial financing is subject to some government restriction. Many of these regulations are designed to keep business competitive, while others protect the economy and the consumer. But, in the context of business performance, the thing to remember is that all of these controls are applied equally to all the member firms of an industry; no one is placed at a particular disadvantage. The fact that the razor-blade industry is forbidden to finance and market its product in a given way doesn't reduce the quantity of razors purchased or the amount of business the industry does. So an increase in government regulation is no proof that honest businessmen are being prevented from developing their enterprise as fast as their ingenuity and resources will permit.

As for your charge that liberal legislation has given labor

leaders the power to dictate wages and production standards to the detriment of business, it just isn't true. There are few unions in the country more powerful or better organized than the United Auto Workers; they have succeeded in improving the standard of living and the working conditions of their members markedly over the past quarter of a century. But look at the auto industry; it's booming as never before. Profits are at a record high and so is new investment. General Motors might prefer to pay its workers less, but there is no indication that union demands have kept GM from growing spectacularly.

It is also interesting to note that many businessmen are beginning to favor liberal measures for stimulating and stabilizing the economy. It was no coincidence after the exceptional economic growth in the Kennedy-Johnson administrations that many of the nation's leading businessmen supported Lyndon Johnson in the last presidential election. In a recent issue of *U. S. News and World Report* a survey of businessmen and bankers across the nation showed that the American business community is steadily coming to accept the new liberal economics as essentially sound. Don't misunderstand me, most of them do not consider themselves liberals; but a large proportion of them are willing to concede that liberal techniques for managing the economy, such as deficit spending and a tax cut without reducing government spending, are working.

As you say, the business sector ought to know what is good for it—and I just do not hear many complaints these days. Why should businessmen complain? Business performance and conditions have never been better. Liberals can be proud of the expansion of free enterprise that has taken place over the past three decades, and we have every reason to expect it to continue in the future.

• *Big Government and Big Labor together are destroying the small businessman.*

CONSERVATIVE: But that expansion you brag about has been limited almost exclusively to big business. The giant corporations have been able to adjust to an economy dominated by Big Government and Big Labor. It's the small proprietorships—the little corner groceries and family firms—that have lacked the resources to fight back and have been pulled under. Liberal preoccupation with hard figures and statistics has obscured this very real human and spiritual loss to the country.

Part of the American dream since the landing of the Pilgrims has been the opportunity to be self-employed, to be your own boss. Men have traditionally scrimped and saved in this country in the hope of buying their own farm, shop, or factory. The chance to become an independent businessman has served not only as an effective economic incentive, but it has been the source of grass-roots political and civic activity. The self-employed man has always experienced a particular pride in his community and a sense of responsibility for its development. By allowing small business to die, liberals have sapped local government of its vitality. Big corporations operate and think in national and international terms; a given town is just the location of one of a number of plants or offices. If the town has problems, just move to a new one, they say.

So while your claim of progress appears to be valid in the indices of government reports, it looks very different when driving past the boarded fronts of the little stores and shops which used to line the main street of every town in America. The hundreds of thousands of men and women who used to run these enterprises and who formed the civic backbone of their communities are now lost. They have been replaced by millions of apathetic citizens who put in their 9-to-5 days in the huge, impersonal plants and bureaucracies which now characterize our economy.

LIBERAL: I share many of your regrets over the disappearance of the corner grocery, but let's not permit our disappointment to distort our view of what has happened. Small businesses, particularly small retail concerns, were beginning to fail in great numbers before Roosevelt came to Washington. In his informal history of the "roaring twenties," *Only Yesterday,* published in 1931, the respected journalist Fredrick Lewis Allen could already write:

> While the independent storekeeper struggled to hold his own, the amount of retail business done in chain stores and department stores jumped by leaps and bounds. For every $100 worth of business done in 1919, by 1927 the five-and-ten-cent chains were doing $260 worth, cigar chains $153 worth, the drug chains $224 worth, and the grocery chains $387 worth. Mrs. Smith no longer patronized her "naborhood" store; she climbed into her two-thousand-dollar car to drive to the red-fronted chain grocery and save twenty-seven cents on her daily purchases.

It wasn't Big Government and organized labor that were making it difficult for the small businessman to survive; it was big business, with its greater efficiency and lower prices. The die was cast well before 1933, at a time when the labor movement was still small and ineffective and the federal government was maintaining a hands-off policy toward business.

There is no denying that certain types of small enterprise can no longer survive in this country. At the same time, many new opportunities have opened up in the last third of a century for the man who wants to be self-employed. Automobiles and increased leisure have created a demand for motels, Dairy Queens, drive-ins, bowling alleys, car washes, miniature-golf courses, and service stations. Of course, it takes more money to get started in such an enterprise than it took to stock a family candy store. Liberals realized this, and that is why the federal Small Business Administration makes loans of up to $250,000 to aspiring businessmen with promising prospects who can't obtain credit from commercial banks. For all the weeping conservatives do over the plight of the small businessman, I've never heard you urge any constructive action to improve the situation. Remember, the Small Business Administration was a creation of liberal government.

The conditions facing the small businessman today are very different from those at the turn of the century; there's nothing any of us can do about that. But there is plenty of evidence that the lone entrepreneur who adopts modern management techniques can hold his own against the large national chains. The independent supermarket and drug center are good examples of what I'm talking about. Conservatives have been content to cry about the changes that have taken place. Liberals, through such means as the Small Business Administration, have worked to help the little businessman adjust to these changes. I'm glad you brought this whole issue up, because it contrasts nicely the differing ways in which conservatives and liberals react to national problems.

• *Liberal giveaway programs have made the farm problem worse, not better.*

CONSERVATIVE: What about the "farm problem"? Surely you are not going to tell me that liberal government has been successful in the field of agriculture. By refusing to leave farming alone, liberals have succeeded in creating economic chaos. Anyone who knows anything about agriculture in this country will tell you that the government's policy of price supports and production controls has been a colossal flop. Why on earth did you start such programs? Listen: When federal intervention began during the New Deal, the problem was declining farm incomes.

Today, many farm incomes are still low, and liberal meddling has blessed us with such new difficulties as unmanageable surpluses, high consumer prices, and a huge tax bill of nearly three billion dollars a year for "agricultural income stabilization." This is progress all right, but in the wrong direction.

What's so disturbing is the fact that the solution to our farm problem is obvious and simple. Farm production, like any other production, should be determined by the free market forces of supply and demand. If this were done, output would balance consumption, retail prices would fall, and those who remained on the farms would end up with higher incomes. The point of the matter is that there are more farmers in America today than we need. Nothing is gained by maintaining the inefficient ones at the public's expense. Everyone involved would be much better off if these marginal farmers were encouraged to leave farming and enter fields where their services would be of use.

For people who are constantly talking about economic growth, liberals are in the ironic position of defending the subsidizing of nonproduction. I give you credit for enough intelligence to see this problem clearly. What you've lacked for the last third of a century is the political courage to do anything about it—a characteristic of liberals, which, the record will show, is all too common.

LIBERAL: Your perception of the farm problem is basically sound. We simply have too many farmers. But your solution of letting the market reduce their number would have much wider repercussions than just eliminating the most inefficient producers. By going back to the origins of this whole situation, I can show you what I mean.

As I pointed out earlier, the farmer didn't share in the general prosperity of the twenties. By the time the New Dealers decided something had to be done about agriculture, the forces of supply and demand had cut net farm income to one-third of its 1929 level, which wasn't very high to begin with. The individual farmer reacted by producing more, which only succeeded in pushing prices still lower. According to you, the obvious solution would have been to let the market do its job and drive enough families off their farms until the remaining units could operate profitably. What you seem to forget is that in 1933 one out of every four nonagricultural workers was unemployed. Where were these millions of farmers and their families supposed to go? How were they going to support themselves? If your advice had been followed, there would have been millions more Americans sitting around our cities with nothing to do, living on relief. This would have solved nothing.

Liberals realized that, if farmers were to be kept financially afloat and self-supporting until the day when marginal producers could find employment in nonfarm occupations, a way would have to be found of adjusting farm production to match consumption. Industry, led by a few large corporations in each field and aided by a tradition of consultation and cooperation, was better able to tailor its supply to fit demand. But agriculture consisted of several million somewhat isolated individual producers, a condition of almost perfect competition which made self-induced agricultural cooperation virtually impossible.

The solution decided upon was a domestic allotment plan, which offered farmers a price subsidy in return for their tacit agreement to limit output. In short-run terms, the plan was to raise farm prices until so-called "parity" was achieved; that is, until farm products regained their pre-World-War-I power to command industrial goods in exchange. Domestic allotment worked. Using the period of 1910-14 as representing full parity of one hundred, the ratio of prices farmers received to the prices they paid rose steadily, from fifty-five percent of parity in 1932, to seventy percent in 1934, to ninety percent in 1936.

The program was administered to a great extent by county production-control committees made up of the farmers themselves, who elected their own officers. So the government kept the whole venture as decentralized and democratic as possible. Production controls were determined by national referendum, with each farmer casting an equal vote regardless of the size of his holding. In short, the American farmer was practicing effective self-government.

CONSERVATIVE: But wasn't this a part of the first Agricultural Adjustment Act that was declared unconstitutional by the Supreme Court because these so-called "voluntary" production controls were really compulsory?

LIBERAL: It was, and when the Supreme Court ordered the dissolution of the program in 1936, the farmers' situation began to fall apart again. Still wanting to keep farm prices at or near parity, the Roosevelt administration put together the second Agricultural Adjustment Act, which tried three different devices for raising prices.

To start with, national acreage allotments for certain basic crops were enacted by Congress. This didn't work because most farmers could produce as much as before on less land by using better methods and intensive planting techniques. The second device, setting marketing limits, was considerably more effective. This was the most direct means of price control short of price setting, and it posed the greatest potential threat to individual freedom. For this reason, Congress stipulated that no quota could become effective without the approval of at least two-thirds of the growers of the crops in question.

Finally, a system of price-support loans was initiated which, like the market quotas, is still in use today. Under this plan, the federal government extended loans to the farmer against his crops at a certain percentage of parity—usually between seventy percent and ninety percent. The loan was a nonrecourse type, which meant that if, during the year, the market price exceeded the loan price, the farmer unloaded his harvest on the market and repaid the government the amount of the loan; but if the market price remained below the loan price, the government took over the farmer's crops as surplus and the farmer kept the loan price.

CONSERVATIVE: So far all you have done is explain how liberals subsidized the farmer. None of these measures faced up to the crux of the problem, which is, as we both agree, that there were and still are too many farmers.

LIBERAL: As I said, while heavy industrial unemployment persisted, there was no place for the unneeded farmers to go. With wartime prosperity and the tremendous demand for labor in the defense plants, men began to leave the countryside. In 1933, more than thirty-two million Americans, or twenty-six percent of the U.S. population, lived on farms. By 1945, this number had dropped to 24.5 million, 17.5 percent of the population. During the two decades that have followed, 11.5 million Americans have left their farms for the city and new jobs. Today, only thirteen million people—6.7 percent of the population—are farm residents. So, time has provided the most effective remedy for our farm problem.

Why, you might ask, with the economy booming, don't we speed up this process by allowing unregulated supply and demand to push out the remaining surplus of agricultural producers? The answer is that the resulting upheaval of the economy and the cost to the taxpayers would be much greater than the current price-support bill of 2.7 billion dollars a year.

In the first place, most of the farmers who would be driven into the city by your survival-of-the-fittest solution would have no industrial skills. Since the demand for unskilled labor is practically nil these days, the majority would be forced to live on welfare until they were retrained. Also, many small-town businessmen throughout the country live on the trade of neighboring farmers. Any overnight reduction in the number of farmers would bankrupt a good proportion of these men and add further to the rolls of the unemployed. Lastly, a lot of industry in the United States is agriculturally-related. With the farm population diminishing steadily over the years, farm implement, fertilizer, and feed concerns have been able to make their plans accordingly and adjust to changing conditions by diversification and other means. To abruptly halve the number of farmers would throw these firms into a state of chaos, leading to more business failures and more unemployment. In short, the policy of gradualism which liberals have been following makes sense in both humanitarian and economic terms.

In retrospect, the liberal farm policy has worked even better than most of its supporters expected. The diminishing number of families still on the farm are living better than ever. *Real* income from farming has doubled since 1929 from $1,849 (in 1964 dollars) per farm to $3,656. As I said before, the availability of inexpensive electricity made possible by the Rural Electrification Administration has boosted the farmer's standard of living. Home ownership among farmers has jumped from fifty-seven percent in 1930 to eighty percent today.

The rise in farm production has been so spectacular—one of the reasons for persisting surpluses—that less than seven percent of the populace is presently capable of raising more than enough food to feed the entire country. Crop yields per acre during the Kennedy-Johnson administrations were sixty percent greater than during the Hoover years. To look at it another way, one man-hour in 1929 produced 14 pounds of meat, 1.4 bushels of wheat, or 47 pounds of vegetables. The same amount of time today gives us 21 pounds of meat, eight bushels of wheat, or 70 pounds of vegetables. Soil erosion and exhaustion, which by 1934 had destroyed 100 million acres of our cropland and resulted in the loss of at least half the topsoil from another 100 million acres, have been brought under control by the Soil Conservation Service and programs like the Soil Bank.

Earlier you said something that sounded as though the cost of all of this improvement has been paid by the consumer in the form of higher food prices. Actually, the retail price of food has risen no faster since 1929 than the prices of other consumer items such as clothes. The average American family spends a smaller share of its budget to obtain a nutritive diet today than it did in the years preceding the Depression. All in all, I think this amounts to an impressive liberal record in agriculture.

CONSERVATIVE: And when does this liberal policy of "gradualism" finally terminate—in my lifetime, in my children's lifetime, or never?

LIBERAL: I can't give you an exact date. Here is the problem—judge for yourself. Of the 3.7 million farms in the country, twenty-one percent produce seventy-two percent of the nation's agricultural output. Needless to say, the people who operate these farms are doing well. At the other end of the scale are the forty-four percent of the farms that account for only five percent of the produce. Most of the people who own these farms depend on nonagricultural employment to provide or supplement their incomes; for the most part, this group doesn't warrant any national concern.

To locate the hard core of the "farm problem," we have to turn to the middle thirty-four percent of the farms, which transact twenty-three percent of the business. This group, which relies entirely on farming for its livelihood, have been finding it increasingly difficult to compete with the bigger farms for lack of capital. These are the people that have to be induced either to enlarge their farm operations or to give up farming, if American agriculture is to become entirely self-sufficient. As time goes on, many of the children of these farmers can be counted on to find jobs elsewhere. The federal government has been working to attract industries into these nonproductive agricultural areas through development programs such as the Appalachia project. These unneeded farmers will not disappear overnight, which would be undesirable anyway. It will take time. But, since liberal patience and planning in the field of agriculture have paid off pretty well so far, I think there is every indication that it will continue to work in the future.

- *The burgeoning federal bureaucracy is wasteful and inefficient, and is fast becoming uncontrollable.*

CONSERVATIVE: There is another problem with all of this liberal activity that we haven't touched on yet. To carry out your innumerable welfare and giveaway programs, you've had to create a huge federal bureaucracy. Even a liberal ought to know what this means. If you don't, stop down at city hall some afternoon and watch the show.

Some poor man comes in Friday wanting to purchase a $1.50 dog license. After being shunted from office to office, filling out endless forms, being reprimanded for bending one of the IBM cards, and waiting for forty-five minutes, he is finally confronted by the man who takes the money for dog licenses. Plunking his $1.50 on the counter, secure in the knowledge that he is nearing the completion of this infuriating ordeal, the dog lover is asked to produce his permit from the Zoning Commission. He asks what he has to do to get one. The clerk, impatiently checking his watch, tells him that the Zoning Commission closed fifteen minutes ago and suggests that he come back on Monday between 3:00 and 4:00 P.M. and they'll take care of him. . . . And we wonder why so many dogs run around town without licenses.

Well, the federal government employs about 2.5 million people, so you can imagine what the bureaucracy in Washington is like. Whenever you have an organization that big, the red tape, waste, and inefficiency are tremendous. Add to this the fact that government employees are members of the Civil Service—which means they're almost impossible to fire—and that they lack profit incentive, and you have a good explanation of why federal spending is sky high.

What is even more disconcerting about this federal leviathan is that it has grown out of touch with the people and beyond public control. Most of these entrenched bureaucrats are more concerned with building personal empires than in servicing the country's needs. No one knows exactly what they're doing, and if someone did, what could he do about it? So, in addition to being a shameless waste of the taxpayers' money, the government bureaucracy represents a real threat to our freedom and democratic way of life.

It doesn't take too much probing to pinpoint the blame for this development either. In 1932 the federal government employed 559,000 civil servants. During the last third of a century that number has multiplied about five times. In other words, in order to even attempt to fulfill their promises to the American people, liberals have been forced to fall back on a device which operates on waste and, if not cut down to a reasonable size, could run off with our liberty. The bureaucracy is another excellent example of liberal means defeating liberal ends.

LIBERAL: You imply that the word "bureaucracy" should always have a bad connotation. The country's big corporation executives will tell you that a bureaucracy is the only efficient way to organize a large group of people with many different and specialized tasks to perform. What do you think a bureaucracy is? It's not defined as a means for making red tape. In the most general sense, it's a form of organization, pyramidal in structure, which relies on a division of labor and clear lines of communication and responsibility from top to bottom in an effort to allow maximum administrative efficiency. Just as the assembly line has developed as the most efficient means of mass production, the bureaucracy is unquestionably the best technique for mass management and administration so far devised. Businesses, hospitals, universities, and governments are all run as bureaucracies.

I agree that the federal bureaucracy is big. But before we start making any drastic cuts in its size, it might be interesting to find out what all these bureaucrats are used for. The largest single group is found in the Defense Department, which employs forty-three percent of all federal civil servants. The Post Office Department accounts for another twenty-three percent of the total, and about fifteen percent man the Treasury Department and the

Veterans Administration. Right there you have four-fifths of the entire government bureaucracy occupied with jobs that both conservatives and liberals agree are indispensable. The remaining twenty percent, who work in the other departments and agencies, comprise a group that is smaller than the administrative bureaucracy of General Motors! My point is that bureaucracies, far from being inherently wasteful, are designed for utmost efficiency. Further, we are both agreed on the need for at least eighty percent of the present federal bureaucracy.

CONSERVATIVE: Bureaucracies may not have to be inefficient, but it's common knowledge that if the federal bureaucracy were run like our businesses are, there is not much doubt that the four activities you mentioned could be administered by a lot less people.

LIBERAL: I'm not sure what "common knowledge" you're referring to, but the information I have indicates that the federal bureaucracy is fairly efficient. By efficient, I don't mean there is no waste. Every large concern has some waste. The important question is: How much waste? A look at the Social Security Administration will give you an idea of the federal bureaucracy's performance. Whatever you think of our social-security program, you have to concede that it is a complex operation to administer. Ninety percent of the work force currently participates in this social-security program, as do the millions who are already receiving benefits. It is estimated that in 1966 the Social Security Administration will take in 23.6 billion dollars in contributions and will pay out an equal amount. Yet, despite the vast size of this program, only 2.5 percent of the monies received by the SSA go for administrative costs, which compares favorably with the operating expenses of commercial insurance firms.

In addition, the federal government was among the first to use Automatic Data Processing, which is a tremendous time and labor saver. Computers enable one Veterans Administration employee to process the same number of insurance policies it took five employees to handle ten years ago. By creating inter-agency motor pools, the government has been able to reduce the traveling costs of its employees by about three cents a mile, which saved taxpayers 8.2 million dollars in 1962. A federal incentive program for suggesting means of increasing efficiency within the bureaucracy has been operating since World War II. In 1962 alone, government agencies adopted approximately 104,500 employee proposals at a saving of nearly 65 million dollars. As for your dig that the federal bureaucracy ought to be run as private businesses are run, the man who for the last five years has been at the head of the Defense Department—which employs nearly half of the 2.5 million federal bureaucrats—didn't get there by "polishing up the handle of the big front door." Robert McNamara was president of the Ford Motor Company, and he's applied the most modern methods of cost analysis to make his department as efficient as possible.

Another indication of improved federal efficiency is the recent growth rate of the bureaucracy. Since 1953 the ratio of federal employees to the population as a whole has been *decreasing,* from 16.3 for every 1,000 Americans to 12.7 per 1,000 today. While the population has been increasing 1.5 percent a year and federal activity has been steadily expanded, the bureaucracy has only been growing at one-half of one percent annually. Federal employment as a proportion of all government employment has fallen from 38.4 percent in 1952 to 24.9 percent in 1965. And indications are that it will keep falling.

This should come as no great surprise, because reducing bureaucratic waste has been a continuing liberal campaign. In 1947, Congress appointed a group headed by the late President Herbert Hoover to study the possibilities of increasing federal efficiency through structural reorganization. Of the 273 recommendations made by this first Hoover Commission, the government adopted seventy-two percent. A similar commission was established in 1953 to suggest further ways of improving bureaucratic performance. The old saw about "government inefficiency" may be "common knowledge," but it's simply not correct. Receiving social security may require filling out a lot of forms, but this is only because it is the most effective way we know of processing the records of millions of Americans. Things can always be improved, but this holds as true for General Motors as it does for the government.

Finally, you claim that the public exerts little or no control over the federal bureaucracy, and that, as a result, government agencies have become unresponsive and even dangerous. I don't agree with you that the bureaucracy is fueled on waste, but it does require money to run. And there's only one place this needed money can come from—the U. S. Congress. Before appropriating funds to the various federal departments and regulating commissions, both the House and Senate demand reports of past performance, plans for the current fiscal year and beyond, and cost and efficiency studies. Hearings are held at which bureaucrats have to come before committees familiar with their areas and justify their requests. This power over the purse strings means that Congress can abruptly halt the activity of any agency it or the president has created by simply cutting off the flow of funds. Also, Congress can stipulate as precisely as it wants how a given appropriation must be spent.

The president is the man directly responsible for the bureaucracy's actions. While it is true that more than ninety percent of federal employees are members of the Civil Service, all department and agency directors and major policy-making personnel are appointed by the president. If he's not satisfied with the performance of a certain part of the government, he can appoint new men to head it, a relatively common practice. In the event that a president and Congress fail to exercise their control over the bureaucracy conscientiously, the opposition party can be counted on to capitalize upon this fact in the coming elections, which are never more than two years away.

In other words, the federal bureaucracy is as well directed and responsive to the nation's needs as the president and Congress wish to make it. And since these are all popularly elected officials, if the public isn't happy with the results, it can vote in a new government.

So, in the final analysis, you are going to have to find some other way to criticize liberal government than simply pointing out that it depends on a large bureaucracy. The federal bureaucracy is efficient and responsive, and the facts prove it. I wish I could suggest some new approaches to you, because it has been fun going over the results of liberal performance in this country since 1933. But we've already touched on most of the major points of conservative criticism, and I don't think your case has held up very well. By and large, liberalism has done what it has promised it would do. Liberal positive government has worked well during the last thirty-some years, and it appears to be doing better than ever at present. I don't know of any sounder way to judge a political philosophy than to watch it in action.

5
Foreign policy

The major conservative indictment of American liberalism, which has cropped up in one form or another from Senator McCarthy to Senator Goldwater, is that liberal foreign policy is causing the United States to lose the cold war.

Whether as the result a State Department conspiracy or because of erroneous thinking, conservatives have complained that American policy is "no win," "unimaginative," and will only result in the eventual loss of the free world to the Communists.

Particular points of contention in this area involve Yalta, Korea, Red China, and, more recently, Cuba.

The conservative claim is that, through some form of negligence on the part of the federal government, Communism has been allowed to grow and flourish; and that the United States, once the undisputed world leader, has lost a great deal of its influence and is becoming a world laughing stock.

To refute this charge, the liberal will have to point out some individual situations and see how the facts fit in with the conservative accusations.

• *America is losing the cold war because of our "no win"
foreign policy.*

CONSERVATIVE: If America is defeated from abroad, it will
make little difference whether liberalism has been effective at
home or not. And this is precisely what is happening. Since the
closing days of World War II, we have been locked in a life-and-
death struggle with international Communism which we have
been losing, and losing badly. What is worse, the liberal foreign
policy, or lack of it, that has been governing our international
performance over the last two decades gives no sign of being
able to reverse this catastrophic trend. Some liberals have tried
to protest that things are not really going that badly, but the
facts overwhelmingly contradict them.

At the close of World War II, the United States emerged as
the single greatest power in the history of the world. American
industrial capacity was unmatched; our control of the air and
seas was undisputed; we had an army of 3.5 million men stationed in every corner of the globe; and, most significantly, we
alone possessed the atomic bomb. By contrast, the Soviet Union
came out of the war with much of her industrial complex destroyed, and with nowhere near the military and economic
strength of the United States. Yet, look at what has happened in
the twenty years since V-J Day.

Communist tyranny has enslaved one-third of the earth's
population—one billion human beings! China fell to the Reds in
1949. Puppet regimes manipulated by Moscow and Peiping
have been set up in Poland, Hungary, East Germany, Bulgaria,
Rumania, Albania, Yugoslavia, Czechoslovakia, North Korea,
North Vietnam, Mongolia, Tibet, and ninety miles off our own
shores in Cuba; Laos and South Vietnam appear on the verge
of being added to the list. Vast portions of Asia, the Middle
East, and Africa, which a short time ago were safely in the
Western camp, have turned eastward under the guise of "neu-

tralism." In our own back yard, Castroism is working to cause unrest and is plotting the subversion of our Latin American neighbors. Even the Western Alliance, which withstood the terrible trials of the war and the immediate post-war recovery, is beginning to crumble. France is in the throes of an anti-American campaign, and there is growing talk in England that our staunchest ally may seek to assume a neutral position in international politics. In short, Communist influence in the world today is greater and far more dangerous than it was in 1945, while Western influence and prestige have declined everywhere during this same period. If this is what liberals call winning the cold war, I think the time has arrived for a reexamination of the rules of the game.

Every American should be asking himself: Why is the richest and most powerful nation in the world losing the battle for survival to a weaker foe? Why hasn't U.S. economic and military might been able to stem the Communist tide that is inundating one part after another of the free world? The answers to these questions are not difficult to find. We are losing the cold war because liberal policy makers refuse to recognize the true nature of the struggle in which we are engaged. Soviet and Chinese ambitions will not be satisfied with one more satellite here or one more "people's revolution" there. The Communists' program is world domination and the destruction of capitalism—nothing short of this will do. Every move by Moscow and Peiping is calculated to further this aim. Consequently, the "peaceful coexistence" with Communism preached by liberal statesmen and politicians is a dangerous pipe dream which fails to face up to the realities of the situation.

The simple truth is, we are at war with the Communists to determine which system will prevail: theirs based on tyranny, or ours founded on freedom. There is nothing "cold" about this war; it's an all-out fight to the finish. By failing to understand or acknowledge this fact of the international situation, liberals have pursued a foreign policy which lacks the means for defeating the enemy. The best example of this liberal "no win" approach is the State Department's "containment" policy, adopted by President Truman and faithfully followed by his successors. Essentially this policy is designed to preserve the *status quo*. It is entirely defensive, defaulting all initiative to the Communists. The United States has repeatedly refused to take the offensive, which is another way of saying that we have exerted no effort to win this war.

I'm all too familiar with the liberal line that "wars aren't won in a nuclear age," from which liberals conclude that some way must be found of accommodating ourselves to the Communists. However much liberals might wish otherwise, there is only one alternative to victory, and that is defeat. We want to avoid a nuclear war, but, as Munich has taught us, appeasement is not the way. Only by adopting a firm, single-minded policy designed to defeat Communism—an offensive and not a defensive strategy—can we hope to deter nuclear destruction. For the United States has the strength to be victorious. What we have lacked is the resolve and the courage. Defeat is not yet inevitable. But, unless we abandon liberal policies quickly, our grandchildren will be forced to ponder our mistakes in a Communist world.

LIBERAL: I happen to be one of those liberals you referred to who believes America is doing reasonably well in the cold war. This is not to say we haven't made mistakes or that there are no aspects of our policies, past and present, open to criticism; but the changes I might suggest would have little in common with your attacks on this country's international performance.

You claim that the evidence "overwhelmingly" demonstrates that the United States is losing the world to the Communists. Let's take a look at how things stand. Before World War II had even ended, the Soviet Union had imposed its control upon Poland, Hungary, Rumania, Bulgaria, Albania, and East Germany, as the Red army drove westward to defeat Hitler. Yugoslavia was already under the Communist control of Marshal Tito, and Czechoslovakia was living in the shadow of Soviet troops. The only way we could have forced the Soviets out of Central and Eastern Europe would have been to declare war on Russia and order our soldiers on to Moscow. Our need to conclude the war in the Pacific, which was still raging at that time, the massive size and strength of the Red army, and the fact that both sides were exhausted after the long and bloody struggle with the Nazis, combined to make such an action unthinkable. We could have attempted to bomb the Soviets out of these areas, but liberation by means of devastation doesn't make much sense. We might have pushed the Red army out of Hungary, but if this meant leveling the country in the process, we would hardly have done the Hungarians a great service.

When the surrender of the Japanese permitted us to return our attention to Europe, three things were clear: Eastern and part of Central Europe were firmly under the thumb of Stalin, Western Europe was prostrate and unable to protect itself against possible Soviet aggression, and internal Communist takeovers were threatened in France, Italy, and Greece. The Truman administration acted decisively, assisting the Greek government to stabilize its shaky position and defeat the Communist guerrillas, and devising the Marshall Plan and the North Atlantic Treaty Organization (NATO) for the reconstruction and defense of Western Europe as a whole.

From our vantage point today, it's clear that these efforts were immensely successful. The Soviets have not gained any European soil since the war's end; in fact, they withdrew from the half of Austria they had occupied in the course of the war. Western Europe has been completely rebuilt and its economies are booming. Communism in France and Italy has declined to the point where it no longer represents a significant danger. Furthermore, Western Europe now possesses the potential to become a third great superstate, capable of swinging the balance of global power decisively to the advantage of the Western world.

On the Communist side of the Iron Curtain, developments have been moving in another direction. Since the death of Stalin, the satellite countries have been increasingly asserting their independence from Moscow. The Soviets' plans to impose their system permanently on these nations is failing, with no sign of reversal in sight. What control they have retained appears to be based exclusively on the presence of Soviet military might; and in time of crisis, the Kremlin cannot confidently count on support from any of her satellites.

Who is winning the cold war in Europe? We are. The growing demand for independent policies in Western Europe testifies to our success in revitalizing that area, while the spreading restiveness and autonomy to the east attests to the Soviets' failure to achieve their ends.

Recognizing by the end of 1948 that their efforts to expand into Europe were being effectively blocked, the Communists shifted their attention to the Far East. It was here that we suffered our biggest setback of the cold war, the loss of the Chinese mainland to the Reds. Unfortunate as it was, it was beyond the power of the United States to prevent it. Chiang Kai-shek's Nationalist army didn't lack arms or other military supplies in its fight with the Communists. We gave Chiang all the aid he needed, and his troops were consistently better equipped than Mao's tattered volunteers. Chiang lost China—and he himself has admitted this—because he failed to win the support of the mass of the Chinese people. He was unable to identify his cause with the aspirations of the majority, and they either opposed him outright or became indifferent to the outcome of the struggle. To make matters worse, Chiang's military strategy, against the protests of his American advisors, was unsuited to the guerrilla warfare being waged by the Communists.

We might have delayed Mao's victory had we taken over direct supervision of the Nationalist armies and committed several million of our own troops to the struggle; but this would have been foolhardy and perhaps fatal. Diverting the preponderance of our military strength to the Far East would have left a still prone Western Europe, our top priority for protection against Communist aggression, vulnerable to Soviet aggression. Moreover, to defeat the Communists decisively would have required our attempting to conquer and occupy most, if not all, of China, the folly of which the Japanese had demonstrated a few years earlier. Our atomic monopoly, which was about to be broken by the Soviets, was of no use since there was nothing strategic to bomb. In short, China was a good example of a situation in which forces were at work that we were incapable of controlling.

For the last fifteen years the cold war has been contested mainly in the underdeveloped parts of the world—the Middle East, Africa, Southeast Asia, and Latin America. Owing to its lack of unity, political instability, economic stagnation, and cultural heterogeneity, each of these regions is a power vacuum which could be expected to remain so for some time if left to itself. However, as we learned in the immediate aftermath of World War II, Communist power will attempt to flow into such voids. To prevent the day when Americans and Western Europeans would wake up to find themselves dangerously isolated in a Red world, the United States has been working to create situations of strength and stability in these areas. Not all of our efforts have met with success, and we still have a lot to learn. But, relative to the Communists, we've been doing quite well.

The problems we face in this new phase of the cold war are much different and more complex than those we encountered in Western Europe. To start with, all of the underdeveloped nations except those in Latin America have emerged from Western imperialism or colonialism since World War II. Your remark that these nations were once "safely in the Western camp" ignores the fact that they were there as a result of compulsion, not of choice. Their experiences have left nearly all of them with a deep distrust and fear of the West, which has presented the Communists with a significant initial advantage.

In addition, these recently independent states are commonly characterized by the extreme poverty, illiteracy, and malnutrition of their peoples. In itself, there is nothing new about their abject condition. Most of the world has existed in a state of material deprivation since the beginning of history. What is revolutionary is the sudden awakening of the masses of the underdeveloped areas to the fact that their suffering is not "a fate ordained by God" but a man-made one. They are no longer willing to acquiesce to their poverty. Riding this wave of "rising expectations," their leaders are desperately seeking to industrialize their nations and to build modern, productive economies—and they want to accomplish this *now*.

The primary goal of our foreign policy is to build a world in which America is secure. This means an Africa, Middle East, Southeast Asia, and Latin America free from Sino-Soviet control. Achieving this does not require that the nations of these regions have pro-Western governments, nor that they employ democratic and capitalistic techniques in managing their affairs. Our aim is to provide them with alternatives to the exclusive reliance upon Soviet or Chinese aid, advice, and methods. The challenge is to convince the leaders and people of the underdeveloped areas that Communism is neither the only way nor the best way to achieve the economic advances they desire. Military strength plays a part in this competition as a means of keeping the Communists from imposing their domination on a country by force. However, economics and social politics are the weapons with the greatest potential impact. Our skill in handling these weapons will ultimately determine the kind of world we live in.

In other words, the measure of our success is not the number of miniature Americas that result. Rather, it is the number of truly independent nations established that are able to meet the demands of their peoples for progress and social justice.

Having said this, let's take a look at how the United States has done to date in this crucial theater of the cold war. The first Soviet attempt to gain a foothold in the underdeveloped world came in the Middle East. In June 1945 the Russians demanded the cession of several Turkish districts along the Soviet border and a strong hand in the administration of the Dardanelles Straits. Pressure on Iran was initiated in 1946, when the Russians refused to pull back their troops from the northern part of that country. However, President Truman's threats of American action forced them to withdraw their ultimatums from Turkey and their troops from Iran.

CONSERVATIVE: Let me digress for a minute. If threats of American power were so effective in the Middle East right after the war, why wasn't this same tactic employed to drive the Reds out of Central and Eastern Europe?

LIBERAL: You can't make a valid comparison between the Soviet position in Europe and her adventures in the Middle East. The eastern half of Europe was the Soviet Union's great prize from a war that had cost her millions of lives. Most of the Red army was stationed there, and Soviet puppet governments existed in nearly all of the satellites at that time. The Middle East was clearly of secondary interest to the Russians, and their probes there were probably as much to test American determination to defend the non-Communist world as anything. To have gotten involved with the United States in Turkey and Iran would have meant risking too much for too little. But this is no reason to conclude that the Soviets could have been intimidated into abandoning their share of Europe; for here the stakes were very high.

Subsequent Soviet attempts to extend their influence into the Middle East haven't met with much more success. When imminent coups threatened Lebanon and Jordan with Moscow-oriented governments in 1958, the United States and Britain intervened to quash them. Gamal Abdou Nasser, President of the United Arab Republic, remains the only major anti-Western spokesman in the area. However, it should be added that, while Nasser has often proclaimed the Soviet line, he has also outlawed the Communist Party in Egypt. In short, the Communists have little to show for their efforts in the Middle East.

In Africa, the chaos and power vacuum created by the rapid withdrawal of the European colonial powers since World War II have provided the Communists with a wealth of opportunities, but in most cases they have been unable to take advantage of them. For a while things seemed to be going their way in the Congo; however, at this point, the Communist-backed rebels appear thoroughly beaten. The two nations boasting the greatest economic progress in Black Africa in recent years—the Ivory Coast and Nigeria—have been relying exclusively on Western methods and support. Ghana and Algeria have frequently mouthed Moscow's pronouncements on world affairs, but the former is a member of the British Commonwealth and the latter retains strong economic ties with France. Of late, the Chinese have enjoyed greater success in Africa than the Soviets, gaining some influence in Mali, Tanzania, and several other West African states.

Instability remains the dominant factor in Africa, so anything is still possible. But the statement that we are losing the cold war on the Dark Continent is simply unsupported by the facts.

The United States has encountered its gravest difficulties in Asia. With Chiang Kai-shek's exodus to Formosa, our strategy became one of containing China much as we had blocked the way to Soviet expansion in Western Europe. To aid us in carrying out this task, we have worked to build strong, friendly governments in Japan, South Korea, Formosa, and the Philippines. The Communists' first attempt to push us out of Asia came in 1950, in Korea. But several years of hard fighting by United States and United Nations troops succeeded in defeating this effort.

At that point, the center of action shifted to Southeast Asia, where both sides have met with mixed results. Our aim has been to create a belt of independent states in this area that would not be subject to Peiping's control. By the time we became directly involved, North Vietnam was already behind the Bamboo Curtain. Since then, things have looked up somewhat.

With British assistance, the Communist guerrillas in Malaya were decisively beaten. Burma and Thailand have reasonably stable governments which have avoided Chinese domination. Laos, which seemed certain to fall to the Communists a few years ago, has somehow remained in a precarious state of neutralist limbo. Cambodia and Indonesia have become increasingly anti-American, which appears to be a consequence of their conclusion that the United States will not be able to maintain its influence in Asia. Understandably, they don't want to be caught on the losing side for fear this would weaken their chances of remaining independent of China.

The key to the future development of Southeast Asia may well be South Vietnam. This is not because the loss of this territory would automatically lead to Chinese control of the entire area, but because the situation presents the opportunity for us to teach an important lesson and to learn an equally important one. We must demonstrate to China that she will not be allowed to extend her influence militarily. For, if the Chinese are not convinced of the impossibility of this approach, we can expect armed conflict elsewhere in Asia.

At the same time, we must learn that military resistance is futile without the economic and social policies to strengthen the areas we are defending. It is not enough to tell a Vietnamese peasant that Communism is evil if the only alternative we leave him is a corrupt, despotic government in Saigon. If you are living in terrible poverty and someone—the Communists, in this case—promises you land reform and greater freedom, what have you got to lose by giving another system a try? If it turns out to be a false promise, you're no worse off than before. In other words, ways must be found of giving the peoples of these Southeast Asian nations a stake in the existing order. If we fail, we have no reason to expect them to help us contain the Chinese.

So our success as a teacher and as a student will have a great deal to do with the development of Asia in the decade ahead. The final outcome is still anybody's guess.

Latin America has presented us with a still different problem. Since it is located on our doorstep, we have often succumbed to the temptation to treat this continent to the south as if it were our own property. The half-century preceding Franklin Roosevelt's Good Neighbor policy was marked by numerous direct interventions by the United States Marines and the continued use of "dollar diplomacy" to control the affairs of South America, Central America, and the Caribbean. Needless to say, this has left a heritage of "anti-Yankee" sentiment which cannot be expected to disappear overnight.

Unlike the rest of the underdeveloped world, most of the nations of Latin America have exercised self-government for a century or more. Unfortunately, these governments have usually been reactionary military dictatorships, serving the interests of small, wealthy land-owning classes. The lot of the average peasant and of the urban laborer has remained desperate, with virtually no improvement generated through the existing political structure. As the "revolution of rising expectations" has begun to spread across the Southern Hemisphere, the United States has been confronted with the alternatives of either helping these people realize their demands for political reform and a more just distribution of wealth or of defaulting these nations to the Communists. Change is inevitable. The only question is whether it will be revolutionary, as the Communists are hoping, or evolutionary, as we prefer.

The approach we have selected for bringing about orderly social and economic change is embodied in the late President Kennedy's Alliance for Progress. A United States-Latin American partnership, it is designed to prove to the peoples of Central and South America that their lives can be improved without resorting to the Communist-supported "radical solution." Substantial financial and technical aid is being offered to those governments that are willing to undertake needed reforms and to channel the benefits of this aid to their impoverished majorities. Again, the key to success is not military, but economic and social.

As in the other parts of the underdeveloped world, the results of the United States-Soviet competition in Latin America have been inconclusive. The Communists did manage to set up a government in Guatemala in the early 1950's, but it was quickly toppled by an American-directed counter-coup. British Guiana had a Marxist prime minister for several years, but he was voted out of power in 1964. Unquestionably, the Communists' most dramatic victory has been Cuba. However, Castroism has enjoyed very limited success on the South American mainland. Guerrilla movements are afoot in several countries, but so far they have been unable to win control of any government. The most hopeful sign for the West has been the emergence of democratic-socialist parties, such as Chile's Christian Democrats. They represent the middle road of democratic reform which the United States would like to see take hold throughout the continent.

There's no denying that our policies in Latin America have often left much to be desired and that we must work to improve them while there is still time. But to say that we have lost or are losing the cold war here simply isn't confirmed by the realities of the situation.

After surveying the state of the cold war in Europe, the Middle East, Africa, Asia, and Latin America, I don't see the basis for your claim that the Communists are defeating us. It is true that we're doing better in certain places than in others; and we have made many mistakes, some of them serious. But remember, the Communists have also shown themselves to be less than infallible. Taking all factors into account, we are doing reasonably well. Mind you, America can still lose this struggle for survival. To maximize our chances for victory, we must continue to reevaluate the nature of this competition and to develop improved techniques for fighting it. And this is precisely what liberal government is trying to do. Our basic disagreement seems to be over the proper definition of victory in the cold war. The ultimate goal of our foreign policy is to create a world in which America will be secure.

CONSERVATIVE: Conservatives don't take issue with this. All we are saying is that, as long as Communism is allowed to flourish anywhere in the world, America will remain in constant danger. Therefore, any foreign policy seeking to insure our security must hold the elimination of Communism as its primary objective, and liberal foreign policy does not.

LIBERAL: I stand corrected. Our disagreement is primarily over the most effective *means* to victory. Obviously, a direct attack upon the Soviet Union is not the way either to eliminate Communism or to change it so that it ceases to be a threat. Such an action would only trigger the nuclear annihilation of both sides, just as a Soviet assault on the United States would signal the end of Western society as we know it, or would like it. Those people who believe that the United States can always be the aggressor without ever being retaliated against are operating under a dangerous delusion. Therefore, any policy which considers preemptive war against a nuclear enemy cannot be labeled "win."

Liberal cold war strategy, like any battle strategy, consists of defensive and offensive tactics. Containment, as you correctly pointed out, is essentially defensive. Its aim was initially to keep the Soviets from pushing the Iron Curtain westward across Europe in the immediate post-war period. With the virtual disappearance of this threat, our containment policy has been restyled to prevent Chinese expansion in Asia and the establishment of Sino-Soviet controlled areas in the underdeveloped world. Part of this defense relies on a flexible military deterrent which has succeeded in convincing the Communists that total war would be suicide, and which is attempting to demonstrate that limited aggression will be equally futile. In the underdeveloped countries we have found it necessary to supplement this deterrent with economic and social programs capable of creating stable, productive states that will not be vulnerable to Communist propaganda and subversion.

American foreign policy also has numerous offensive features. Recognizing that military action against Russia and Eastern Europe would be as self-defeating as a Soviet attack on the United States or Western Europe, we have designed more subtle means for weakening the Communist world and reducing its ability to challenge our security.

Liberal policy makers have long been aware that Communism has ceased to be the monolithic movement it was during the 1930's. At that time the Soviet Union stood as the only Communist nation, and Communist parties and front groups in other countries looked to Moscow for their directives. In recent years this situation has radically changed. The Communist world has been torn by constant bickering and fighting over ideological and nationalistic differences. Most dramatic has been the Soviet-Chinese split, which many experts view as irreconcilable. Less publicized, but equally significant disagreements have arisen in Eastern Europe, where Yugoslavia's Marshal Tito has constantly declared his independence from Moscow, and where some of the other satellites have begun to do the same.

As the rifts in the Communist bloc widen and deepen, the West is presented with increasingly attractive opportunities for gain. We have been supplying military and economic aid to Yugoslavia to help her sustain her growing autonomy. President Johnson's policy of "building bridges to Eastern Europe" is designed to give the other Iron Curtain countries the commercial alternatives they must have in order to escape their economic dependence on the Soviet Union. The response in Poland, Hungary, and Rumania has been extremely encouraging. Increased stability in Southeast Asia may eventually provide us with a chance to exploit Soviet and Chinese differences more effectively. Dividing the enemy has traditionally been a useful offensive tactic, and our foreign policy has been employing it with good results.

However, while our playing upon divisions in the Sino-Soviet camp weakened the Communists, it did nothing to alter their revolutionary goal of world domination. Some way, short of militarily destroying the Soviet Union and China, had to be found of actually changing the nature of Communism. This is where containment reentered the picture. As George Kennan, the principal architect of America's containment policy, explained prophetically in 1947:

[A successful containment strategy] has it in its power to increase enormously the strains under which Soviet policy must operate, to force upon the Kremlin a far greater degree of moderation and circumspection than it has had to observe in recent years, and in this way to promote tendencies which must eventually find their outlet in either the break-up or the gradual mellowing of Soviet power. For no mystical, messianic movement—and particularly not that of the Kremlin—can face frustration indefinitely without eventually adjusting itself in one way or another to the logic of that state of affairs.

In effect, Kennan was restating the old thesis that, within an authoritarian or totalitarian society, certain frustrations arise that can be relieved only by being channeled into an aggressive and expansionist foreign policy. Successful Soviet containment would prevent this expansion, aggravating the internal tensions in such a way that they would either destroy the Soviet system or force the Soviet leaders to placate the domestic dissatisfaction. Since Soviet leaders presumably preferred to remain in power, and since a relaxation of international tensions was a necessary condition for coping with their domestic difficulties, they would be forced to moderate their foreign policy. Thus, by blocking Soviet expansion, the United States could force the Kremlin to abandon its revolutionary aims and to arrange some sort of working agreement with the West.

Almost two decades later, the facts appear to be bearing out Kennan's analysis. Under Khrushchev, demands for a higher standard of living and a greater emphasis on consumer rather than military products began to surface in the USSR. Since the Cuban missile confrontation in the fall of 1962 taught the Soviet leaders that their efforts to bully and bluff the United States into a corner would go unrewarded, there are many indications that the Kremlin is increasingly fixing its attention upon holding on to what it's got and slowly surrendering its dreams of a world-Communist empire in the foreseeable future. This does not mean that we can afford to abandon our vigil, for it may be only a temporary shift in the Soviet position. But, on the other hand, if Soviet pleas for peaceful coexistence are sincere, we will have achieved a major turning point in the cold war.

In addition to our attempts to take advantage of differences within the Communist world and the possible transforming effects of containment, the United States employs propaganda, espionage, the training of anti-Communist guerrillas, and a whole array of conventional offensive tactics to defeat the Communists. To claim that liberal foreign policy is "no win," reflects a very limited knowledge of America's cold war strategy and actions over the past twenty years.

In fact, if any approach to our struggle with the Communists lacks a capacity for creating a world in which freedom to differ is secure, it is the conservative approach. Your tendency to view international affairs in simplistic, black-and-white terms causes you to miss opportunities and to present advantages to the Communists. For example, the conservative appraisal of Communism as a single-minded conspiracy to destroy capitalism blinds you to the very real differences that exist between the various Communist nations. For all of your distrust of the Communists, you're too quick to take them at their word, ignoring power struggles within the bloc and national ambitions and jealousies. Simply to operate on the proposition that "all Communists are evil," reduces the available offensive options tremendously.

Conservative unwillingness to recognize the legitimacy of neutralism also plays directly into Communist hands. By telling the underdeveloped nations that they must either be "for us or against us," as the late Secretary of State John Foster Dulles often did, you drive these recently independent countries with their strong anti-Western fears into the Communist camp. To understand their position, all you have to do is recall America's passion for neutrality and "nonentanglement" which lasted for more than a century after the American Revolutionary War.

In your impatience for "total victory" now, you would place this country at a great disadvantage and seriously compromise our security. Communist cold war strategy, whether you're speaking of the Soviets or the Chinese, is predicated on long-range plans and extreme patience. American impulsiveness would either give the Communists the opening they've been waiting for or lead to an atomic exchange and the destruction of our society. This is what I would characterize as a truly "no win" approach to foreign policy.

• *Yalta, Korea, and Cuba are good examples of American losses through liberal weakness and indecision.*

CONSERVATIVE: Your whitewash of United States foreign policy neatly glosses over the prime examples of the soft-thinking indecisiveness and timidity that have constantly characterized our behavior in the cold war. Three episodes, in particular, afford real insight into America's approach to this struggle with the Communists: the Yalta conference, the Korean stalemate, and Fidel Castro's takeover of Cuba.

At Yalta, liberals repeated their 1919 Versailles performance of winning the war only to lose the peace. Naïvely believing that Stalin could be trusted, the United States approved Soviet occupation of the eleven Eastern European countries. As though this were not enough, Roosevelt also allowed the Soviet Union to annex the eastern half of Poland and agreed to coalition governments for Yugoslavia and Poland, with Communists holding the key posts. While Stalin did promise to permit free elections in all Soviet-occupied areas, nothing was ever done to make him live up to his word. At the same time, the foundations for the fall of China were laid as Roosevelt acceded to Russian demands for territory and increased influence in Asia. In short, liberal failure to understand the nature of Communism at Yalta resulted in the sellout of seven hundred million Europeans and Asians to Red slavery.

Korea was a case where, with victory in our hands, liberal lack of confidence in American power caused us to accept a humiliating stalemate. When United States forces had driven the Red Chinese and North Koreans back to the 38th Parallel (the boundary between North and South Korea), General Douglas MacArthur vigorously urged President Truman to give him the authorization to push forward for the unification of Korea. In the process of decisively winning this war, MacArthur recognized the opportunity to "severely cripple and largely neutralize China's capability to wage aggressive war and thus save Asia from the engulfment otherwise facing it." The general courageously called for a naval blockade of the Chinese coast, air bombardment of China's industrial complex and military installations, and reinforcement of United States forces with Chinese Nationalist troops, making possible a counterinvasion of the mainland by Chiang Kai-shek.

If MacArthur had been listened to, there seems little doubt that today Korea would be united under a non-Communist government, and that China would be either much weaker or actually returned to Nationalist control. But, true to form, when the chance for a major American breakthrough appeared, liberals lost their nerve and were content with restoring the *status quo.* "Too great a risk," State Department spokesmen cautioned. "The Soviet Union might get involved." Despite our military superiority to the Soviets and Chinese, we refused to seize the initiative and take advantage of our power. So, after one year of bitter fighting and thousands of American deaths, we were no further ahead than when the North Koreans had first invaded.

Infuriating and inexcusable as Yalta and Korea were, Cuba presents the classic case of American indecision and weakness in the cold war. For here we were not dealing with a nuclear power like the Soviet Union, or a vast, populous nation like China, but with a tiny, impotent island practically a stone's throw off our own shores.

Our first mistake was allowing ourselves to be taken in by Castro's loud denials of any Communist sympathies. But, in itself, there was nothing irreversible about this erroneous judgment. When it became unavoidably clear that Castro was nothing but a Kremlin puppet in our midst, we should have acted promptly and decisively to liberate the island and help the Cuban people regain their freedom. Instead, the United States government did nothing. As Barry Goldwater noted in his candid discussion of the situation in *Why Not Victory?*:

> In the Cuban crisis we have moved with an astounding timidity and indecision. We were mesmerized by the intellectual theory of non-intervention while Castro went on shouting insults, confiscating our property, jailing our citizens, and "courting" the deadliest enemy this world has ever known until the moment he admitted he is and always has been a Communist. Our posture before the world has been that of a paralyzed, confused giant only vaguely aware of the danger confronting him—a giant possessed of all the strength necessary to meet the danger but unable to decide to use it.

When we finally decided to act, it was in such a half-hearted and hesitant fashion that we succeeded only in strengthening Castro's prestige and in making ourselves the laughingstock of the world. If we had supplied those brave Cuban refugees in the Bay of Pigs with the kind of support we had promised, Cuba would likely be a free country today. However, an eleventh-hour decision by the White House to withdraw air support of the invasion sealed the project's doom. And as we sit here talking now, more than half a decade after Castro's takeover, Cuba remains a defiant Communist base for the subversion of Latin America—a mere ninety miles from Miami!

If the Communists can get away with this, no wonder Mao Tse-tung derides the United States as a "paper tiger" and Moscow and Peiping grow bolder by the day. The Communists respect one thing and one thing only—power; and for the past twenty years, from Yalta to the Bay of Pigs, liberals have exhibited a studied unwillingness to invoke America's great economic and military power in the cold war. This is why conservatives are convinced that the United States will lose the world to the Communists unless men with more courage and a deeper determination to win are placed in control of our foreign policy.

LIBERAL: In my opinion, the examples you cited illustrate not so much the weaknesses of American foreign policy as the conservatives' failure to study recent history carefully. To show you what I mean, let's take another look at Yalta, Korea, and Cuba.

To evaluate the Yalta conference and its effects upon the map of Europe, it's essential to keep the sequence of events straight. On February 4, 1945, the day the negotiations at Yalta began, all of Eastern Europe except for part of Czechoslovakia was occupied by the Red army, which was already well into Germany. By contrast, United States forces were running into a last-ditch Nazi offensive at the Battle of the Bulge, and they hadn't yet crossed the Rhine. To say that Roosevelt "sold out" Eastern Europe makes as much sense as accusing Stalin of having "sold out" Italy and France. Europe was divided at the end of the war primarily on the basis of which areas the American and Red armies had occupied, respectively, by V-E Day, not on the basis of any United States-Soviet deals. And we should consider ourselves lucky that geography granted us the more industrialized and advanced half of the continent in a war that saw the Soviets suffer the heaviest losses.

As for the charge that FDR permitted the Communists to form coalition governments to their advantage in Eastern Europe, it is just another case of conservative chronological confusion. Poland is a good example. At the time of Yalta the Soviets were in control of Poland, and they had already set up their own puppet government. At our insistence, they made concessions and agreed to reorganize the government to include democratic elements. Therefore, there could hardly have been a sellout of democratic Poland, since there was no democratic Poland to begin with.

To understand the agreements concerning Asia, it's necessary to go back to the war with Japan. Our military experts predicted that the fighting in the Pacific might drag on until 1947, at the cost of up to a million American casualties. Furthermore, it wasn't yet known whether the A-bomb would actually work. At the same time, no one would deny that it was FDR's obligation to defeat the Japanese with as little loss of American life as possible, which meant bringing the Russians into the war to tie up Japanese troops stationed on the Asian mainland. To think that a refusal to deal with Stalin at Yalta would have prevented the Red army from flowing into the power vacuum that was developing in Asia, ignores the fact that we had no available troops to stop them. For that matter, in the absence of the Yalta agreements, Stalin might have made a deal with Japan to split up Asia and remain neutral.

While Roosevelt didn't surrender anything of significance at Yalta which he could have denied Stalin, he obtained some major concessions from the Soviets. They accepted the American voting formula for the United Nations; they allowed France to administer a portion of Germany; they promised to permit free elections in the areas they had occupied; they pledged to sign a pact of friendship with Chiang Kai-shek—not Mao; and they agreed to let China retain full control over Manchuria. Weighing the concessions made by both sides, Yalta was clearly a diplomatic triumph for the United States and Britain. The fact that the Russians didn't keep some of their promises after Yalta is no reflection on the content of the agreements; and it certainly doesn't prove that any "sellout" or betrayal was involved. Even if the Russians hadn't initially agreed to hold elections in Eastern Europe, there's nothing we could have done about it short of declaring war on the Soviet Union.

In other words, Stalin didn't get anything at Yalta that he didn't already have as a result of the Red army's successes against the Nazis. On the other hand, we were able to bring World War II to the quickest possible conclusion and were given the opportunity to ascertain Soviet plans for the post-war period. Roosevelt had correctly perceived that, unless the United States and Russia could cooperate after Germany's defeat, world peace would not be secure. An honest attempt had to be made to work with Stalin to determine his real intentions, and Yalta was the ideal time, because we had little of any importance to lose. Our early discovery that the Soviets still dreamed of world domination was of great strategic importance. We were thereby immediately put on our guard against Soviet aggression and intrigue in those areas, such as Western Europe and the Middle East, where we could effectively bring our power to bear. Whether you examine Yalta in the context of its time or from our own vantage point today, it was clearly an American success.

To my way of thinking, Korea was an even greater success which, had it been followed up properly by the Eisenhower administration, might have resulted in a much stronger American position in Asia today. The North Korean invasion to the south was a test of United States determination to apply the containment policy, that was working so well in Europe, to Communism in Asia. If we had failed to respond to South Korea's pleas for assistance, the result would have been the disintegration of our alliance system and the eventual isolation of the United States. For, had we shown ourselves unwilling or unable to stand by a friend in the face of Communist aggression, our promises to preserve the national integrity and political independence of our allies around the world would have been rendered worthless. Those nations that had depended on us for their protection would be forced to turn to neutralism or Sino-Soviet subservience.

President Truman unhesitantly dispatched United States troops to the Korean peninsula under the flag of the United Nations. Within three months, MacArthur's United Nations forces had driven the invaders back across the 38th Parallel. Believing that the Chinese would not intervene unless directly attacked, the President ordered the general to cross the parallel in an effort to unify Korea. Contrary to expectations, the Red Chinese entered the war in mass and nearly succeeded in pushing the outnumbered United Nations army into the sea. However, after five months of bloody fighting, MacArthur again stood at the 38th Parallel.

This time, Truman gave the signal to halt. Had the President and his advisors suddenly lost their nerve? The possible consequences of attempting to move north again, and of implementing MacArthur's plan for bombing China, indicate that the President acted out of reason, not out of timidity. At worst, these actions would have forced the Soviet Union into the conflict and precipitated World War III. The Sino-Soviet treaty of February 1950 had bound the Soviet Union to come to the aid of China if she were attacked. A refusal to respond to a United States bombardment of China would have destroyed Russia's reputation as a world power, just as a failure to act in Korea would have undermined America's international stature. Also, it should be remembered that the United States no longer held a monopoly on atomic weapons.

At best, the USSR would have remained aloof, and we would have been involved in a war of attrition with the gigantic Chinese army. As General Bradley, Chairman of the Joint Chiefs of Staff, remarked at the time:

> [Nothing would give the Kremlin greater pleasure then the] enlargement of the war in Korea to include Red China. . . . It would necessarily tie down additional forces, especially our sea power and air power, while the Soviet Union would not be obliged to put a single man into the conflict. . . . A "limited war" with Red China would increase the risk we are taking by engaging too much of our power in an area that is not the critical strategic prize.

Finally, MacArthur's strategy was rejected by the Joint Chiefs of Staff because they didn't think it would work. Blockading and bombing China would have only a limited effect, since Mao's armies were supplied from the Soviet Union. The use of Nationalist troops was no more promising, because Chiang had already demonstrated his ineffectiveness on the mainland. In the words of political scientist John Spanier, "MacArthur's strategy would involve us in the wrong war, at the wrong place, at the wrong time, and with the wrong enemy."

Besides, the United States had achieved its primary objective of restoring the 38th Parallel as the boundary between the two

Koreas. South Korea had been successfully defended. The Communist attempt to shatter the Western Alliance, and thereby isolate the United States, had only resulted in the rearming and strengthening of NATO. And, most important, containment had been transplanted to the Far East. We had made it clear that Communist aggression—limited or otherwise—would not be tolerated, no matter where it occurred.

Herein lay the real significance of the Korean War. Prior to the North Korean invasion, we had prepared ourselves solely for the possibility of an all-out Soviet attack on either Western Europe or the United States. To deter such an eventuality, we had developed a strategy of "massive retaliation" which, in effect, warned the Kremlin that any such attack would entail their own destruction. The backbone of this deterrent against total war was the Strategic Air Command (SAC), which kept United States bombers on constant alert at bases circling the Soviet Union. Korea was a clever Communist maneuver to expand without provoking United States massive retaliation. By confronting us with a less than total challenge in an area that wasn't directly related to American security, they left us with the unacceptable alternatives of triggering a nuclear war over a limited objective, or doing nothing—the alternatives of suicide or surrender. Surmising that the United States would not choose to fight World War III unless directly threatened, the Communists believed they had discovered a way of devouring the non-Communist world bit by bit without ever provoking a United States response.

Truman's solution to this American dilemma of suicide or surrender was an increase in the flexibility of our armed forces to enable us to fight limited conflicts wherever they might break out. Korea was our chance to show the Communists that they couldn't expect to get away with these less-than-all-out incursions. By repelling the North Koreans and Chinese, we created a credible deterrent to limited wars which complemented our strategy of massive retaliation. Unfortunately, the Eisenhower administration failed to understand the lesson of Korea, and they returned to an exclusive reliance upon massive retaliation to contain Communism. This is partly why we find ourselves in Vietnam today, trying to reconvince the Chinese that Korea was no fluke. So, far from reflecting liberal indecision and weakness in the cold war, Korea was a sign of United States determination and ability to keep the Communists from realizing their plans of global domination.

As for Castro's takeover of Cuba, the incident you became the most incensed about was easily the least significant of the three examples you cited. However, you are not alone in your feelings. Over the last few years, Communist Cuba has been the source of so much hysteria and so many reckless policy proposals in the United States that it is time we put this island's situation in its proper perspective.

To begin with, Cuba and its six million people represent no direct threat to the United States. That they are situated only ninety miles off our shores is of little consequence; the Soviet Union is only one mile from American territory across the Bering Strait. Furthermore, the conservative cry that a Communist state a stone's throw from Florida is "intolerable" is contradicted by the fact that we have tolerated Castro's Cuba without too much difficulty since 1959. The only real danger Cuba presents lies in its efforts to subvert the other nations of Latin America.

There are two ways we can deal with this danger. The first is to overthrow the Castro regime, either by landing the Marines or by fomenting internal revolution. The question is, will the benefits resulting from military intervention outweigh the costs of such an action? In my opinion, the answer is "no." On the debit side, there is the possibility of a confrontation with the Soviet Union and the certain loss of American lives resulting from an invasion.

CONSERVATIVE: Excuse me. If you follow that kind of reasoning, we can never take a resolute stand against Communist expansion. For every time we say "no" to the Reds or attempt to push them out of an area, we run the risk of initiating World War III or at least spilling some American blood. Callous as it may sound, this is the price of freedom. Americans risked their lives to win independence from England, to preserve the Union, to free the Cubans from Spanish tyranny in 1898, to defeat the Kaiser, and to save the world and democracy from Hitler's madness. Brave men died in those battles, and more will likely have to die if we are to win the cold war. The only "sure thing" that will result from refusing to gamble our immediate safety in this struggle with the Communists is the eventual disappearance of freedom throughout the world. Liberals would do better to base their foreign policy on Patrick Henry's heroic "Give me liberty or give me death," rather than on the cowardly pacifist cry of "Better Red than dead."

LIBERAL: I am not contending that the defense of our freedom doesn't involve risks and the possible loss of lives. However, I do maintain that there are situations in which those risks and losses are justified and situations in which they are not. To fail to make this distinction is to confuse courage with recklessness. The confrontation with the Soviets over the placement of missiles in Cuba was a case where the possibility of triggering World War III had to be accepted. In the eyes of President Kennedy and his advisors, the price we might have to pay for allowing Cuba to arm herself with such weapons was greater than the risk of nuclear annihilation. The United States held its ground and won its objectives.

But I do not believe that the benefits to be gained by overthrowing Castro warrant the chance of a nuclear exchange and American deaths. Our main problems in Latin America are not caused by Castro; as Senator J. William Fulbright has pointed out:

> . . . they are the result of a process of a rapid and profound change in societies which are stubbornly resistant to change. If Cuba were to sink below the Caribbean tomorrow, and if Moscow

were suddenly and miraculously to recall all of its agents in the Western Hemisphere, much of Latin America would still be agitated by unrest, radicalism, and revolution.

There is no question that Castro makes it more difficult for us to solve these problems, but not enough so to justify the possible costs of invasion.

This brings us to the second way of dealing with Cuba, which is to isolate Castro and strengthen Latin America against his subversive efforts. This strikes me as the wisest course, and it has been our government's continuing policy since 1960, with the exception of the Bay of Pigs fiasco.

CONSERVATIVE: Surely you can't deny that the Bay of Pigs was a typical example of liberal indecisiveness and weakness.

LIBERAL: Considering John Kennedy's decisiveness and strength during the Cuban missile crisis, I hardly think his behavior in the Bay of Pigs project can be condemned as "typical." The late President freely accepted full responsibility for the ill-fated attempted invasion. Having been in office only a short time, he was still somewhat unsure of himself and, despite misgivings about the project, allowed it to proceed. He later came to believe that it never should have been launched, and he resumed the policy of building up Latin America's resistance to Communism.

And, so far, although he has certainly given it great effort, Castro has not succeeded in subverting a single Latin American nation. Cuba has been excluded from the Organization of American States, and fifteen member nations have broken off diplomatic relations with the Castro government. By inflating the danger of Castroism completely out of proportion, we have only succeeded in making a minor demagogue appear larger in the eyes of the rest of the world. In short, though Castro is working against United States' interests in the Western Hemisphere, his continued existence should not prevent us from attaining our major objective of helping the peoples of Latin America realize their demands for a better life. In achieving this, we will have deprived Cuban Communism of the opportunity to plant the seeds of revolution elsewhere.

Your analysis of the Yalta conference, the Korean War, and Castroism reveals the persistence of certain dangerous misconceptions in your approach to international affairs. The United States is not omnipotent; we're not capable of controlling everything that goes on in the world. At the same time, while the Soviet Union and Red China are not all-powerful, neither are they "paper tigers." Until more Americans accept these facts, and realize that the conservative call to "get tough with the Reds" is hardly the strategy with which to fight the cold war, we continue to run the risk of pushing the Soviets or Chinese into a corner, with nuclear exchange as the only exit. We can win this contest with the Communists, but only by means of intelligent, flexible, long-range plans. We can win, but not until we rid ourselves of the "old myths that blind us to the realities of our time."

• *Peaceful coexistence is impossible. It is nothing more than a piece of Red propaganda, swallowed hook, line, and sinker by gullible liberals.*

CONSERVATIVE: Liberals are hardly the ones to speak of myths and realities in international affairs. For the most dangerous myth governing United States foreign policy today is the liberal belief in the possibility of "peaceful coexistence" with the Communists. As long as this self-delusion remains the cornerstone of our cold war strategy, America can only expect to stand idly by while the Reds grab one part of the free world after another.

Every Communist statement and action is directed toward one objective, and it's not "peaceful coexistence." The men in Moscow and Peiping have never stopped letting it be known that Communist domination of the world is their ultimate and unyielding goal. As recently as 1961, the new Communist manifesto openly admitted that the "peaceful coexistence of states does not mean renunciation of the class struggle. Peace is the true ally of socialism, for time works for socialism and against capitalism. The policy of peaceful coexistence is a policy of mobilizing the masses and launching vigorous action against the enemies of peace." Yet, despite this unmistakable Communist declaration of intent, most liberals go on deceiving themselves that accommodation with the Reds is possible in some imaginary "twilight zone" between victory and defeat.

As Barry Goldwater put it, the cold war "is a conflict where one side or the other must win, and no amount of wishful thinking can make it otherwise." This is so because we and the Communists are pursuing contradictory ends and hold antithetical concepts of man and his nature. These differences are the ones that distinguish freedom from tyranny and individualism from collectivism. They can never be subject to negotiation or compromise by either side, for they are the very substance of both systems. If a Communist abandons the struggle for world domination, he is no longer a Communist. Likewise, if we barter away our belief in the dignity of the individual, we cease to represent the forces of freedom. Accommodation is impossible. And the sooner liberals accept this reality, the better our chances of victory will be.

LIBERAL: As I understand it, a policy of peaceful coexistence doesn't necessitate or even imply that we or the Communists abandon or compromise our respective values and goals. Peaceful coexistence is simply a mutual agreement to establish certain ground rules for fighting the cold war, aimed at preserving the possibility of a meaningful victory for either side. Liberals don't entertain any notions that this national and ideological struggle we have been waging with the Communists for the past two decades can be reconciled overnight. But we have realized, as have the Soviet leaders, that a military confrontation between the United States and the Soviet Union can only end in the total destruction of both societies; in other words, in defeat for both sides and victory for neither. Peaceful coexistence is a tacit understanding to fight the cold war with nonmilitary means, such as propaganda, foreign aid, and even subversion—anything short of actual armed conflict between the two great nuclear powers.

Such an understanding is not only possible, it is absolutely essential if we are to avoid World War III. Unlike most other international agreements, it involves no formal treaties, no inspections, and no mutual trust. Both parties can be expected to refrain from creating unnecessary military crises, for no other reason than that both are aware that they have nothing to gain and everything to lose by escalating a disagreement or limited conflict into a nuclear war.

Khrushchev did boast in the 1961 manifesto that he would "bury" us, but he didn't mean under a blanket of radioactive fallout. He contended that our grandchildren would live under Communism because he was certain his system would outperform ours in the years to come. He was confident the Soviet Union would supplant the United States as the leading industrial power, and that the Communists would defeat us in the contest for the allegiance of the underdeveloped nations. These claims were not made lightly. The Soviets are as intent as ever on winning the cold war. They do realize, however, that nuclear weapons have forced a shift in the nature of this struggle. And "peaceful coexistence" is the label we've given the deadly earnest—but, hopefully, nonmilitary—United States-Soviet competition that has resulted.

Anyone with confidence in our mixed-enterprise economy and representative democracy ought to welcome this Soviet challenge. For, increasingly, the outcome of the cold war should reflect the relative merits of the competing systems. We will have to maintain the economic growth rate of the Kennedy-Johnson years and refine our social and economic programs in the underdeveloped world if we wish to win. In addition, a way will have to be found to convince the Chinese that armed aggression is self-defeating in an atomic age. But there is every reason to believe that America can succeed at these vital tasks through a combination of imaginative planning and determination.

The conservative charge that peaceful coexistence is tantamount to accommodation or appeasement completely misses the mark. In truth, peaceful coexistence is a policy which both sides have recognized as necessary if anyone is to survive the cold war. For the alternative is a nuclear coextinction which serves nobody's interests.

• *Foreign aid is nothing but a multi-billion-dollar boondoggle, wasting the money of American taxpayers. Everyone knows you can't buy friends.*

CONSERVATIVE: In your discussion of liberal cold war strategy, you have repeatedly stressed the importance of foreign aid. I would think that, after giving away more than 100 billion dollars of the taxpayers' money, liberals would recognize the worthlessness and waste of these handouts. Our "Santa Claus" attitude over the past twenty years hasn't succeeded in making us any more popular in the world. For the truth of the matter is, you can't buy friends. Friends are obtained through mutual respect, something that will never develop as long as half the world is feeding out of our hand. Furthermore, most of our aid is not sent to our allies, but to the so-called "neutralist" countries, and even to avowed enemies, such as Yugoslavia. Only liberal reasoning could devise a program which goes to great expense to strengthen the Communists, who have promised to destroy us.

Besides, the United States assistance that does reach the truly pro-Western nations in the underdeveloped world actually retards their economic growth. From our own history, we know that economic development and progress are dependent upon a vigorous private enterprise system. By giving countries enough aid to maintain themselves at a subsistence level, we only delay the day when they must face up to the problem of generating their own capital, the key to private commercial development. Those promising projects, which are too costly for local interests to underwrite alone, would have no difficulty attracting private investors from the United States and abroad. In other words, by reducing our aid and thereby forcing our friends to rely on their own resources, supplemented by some foreign private capital, we would hasten the industrialization and general economic development of the emerging nations. In addition, an emphasis on self-reliance and away from charity would enable us to earn the kind of respect from the uncommitted people which leads to lasting loyalties and enduring friendships. A drastic cut in our foreign aid program would not only eliminate a waste of tax money that runs into the billions every year, but also represent a big step toward winning the cold war.

LIBERAL: I quite agree that a nation can't buy friends. This is not, and never has been, the purpose of our foreign aid program. Its principal aim is to help other nations create the viable economics needed to eliminate the hunger and misery which Communism so successfully exploits. The assistance we dispense is not charity motivated by any sense of Christian duty or the "white man's burden," although such assistance is consistent with all that is decent and fine in the Western tradition. United States foreign aid is the product of national self-interest. For, if the governments of the underdeveloped nations are unable to satisfy the "rising expectations" of their peoples, the West will soon find itself isolated in a Communist world.

The effectiveness of a carefully planned aid program was demonstrated by the great success of the Marshall Plan. At the end of World War II, much of Europe was a charred wasteland. Millions of people were out of work and unsure of even the meanest necessities of food and shelter. More than half of Britain's factories lay idle, and France's iron and steel production had fallen to less than fifty percent of its pre-war level. Germany existed in a state of complete economic chaos; as late as 1947, a package of cigarettes was the equivalent of a month's wages for the average German worker. Western Europe was on the verge of collapse and, as could be expected, the Communist Party began to gain massive support among the Continental working classes. In the elections after the war the Communist Party polled one-fourth of the vote in France and one-third of the vote in Italy.

If European industry could get back on its feet, prosperity would be forthcoming. But that initial lift had to come from the outside; these nations lacked the means to purchase the commodities needed to start their factories going. America's answer was the Marshall Plan, a massive injection of 12 billion dollars into the economies of Western Europe between 1948 and 1952. This relatively small investment—less than the nation's liquor bill during the same period—returned enormous dividends. Western Europe achieved a remarkable recovery, which was accompanied by the steady diminution of Communist popularity.

Today, the underdeveloped world requires a similar large-scale assistance program. Your case for leaving these new nations to their own resources and to foreign private investment falls down for a number of reasons. To begin with, the countries of Asia, Africa, the Middle East, and Latin America are terribly poor. The internal savings required for sufficient capital accumulation can't be squeezed out of a people living at subsistence level—that is, not without totalitarian controls. Outside private capital cannot be depended on to transform these stagnant agrarian economies into modern industrial economies capable of sustaining their own capital accumulation. Before a society can provide attractive opportunities for private investment, it must have roads, schools, hospitals, and other public facilities and services. These prerequisites to drawing enough foreign private capital to get an economy off the ground are projects which offer little or no financial returns to an investor. Western businessmen understandably prefer the quick and sizeable profits to be earned in the booming American and European economies. In other words, the underdeveloped nations cannot be expected to become self-reliant or to receive large amounts of foreign private capital until public funds are available to create the necessary economic climate.

It requires very little imagination to predict what will happen if we do not provide this needed public capital. The economies of the emerging nations will fail to develop and grow, and may even fall below the subsistence level as a result of their exploding populations. The attendant misery and disillusionment will provide the Communists with the environment in which they operate best. In his *American Foreign Policy Since World War II,* John Spanier describes what can be expected to happen at this point:

> The Communists could then—in fact, they already do—point to the Soviet experience and say: "In 1917, Russia was also underdeveloped, but now, within the space of one generation, we are the second most powerful industrial country in the world. You, too, can be industrialized quickly and live a better life. Just look how fast China is progressing with our help." To people who already suffer from chronic hunger and poverty, it will not matter greatly that the Soviet Union and Communist China achieved industrialization by means of totalitarian governments which brutally squeezed the necessary savings out of the people; the loss of liberty will not mean much to people who have never known it anyway, who have lived for centuries under authoritarian governments, whether domestic or foreign.

If America allows this sequence of events to run its course, we will have lost the cold war by default. The day when "fortress America" was a possibility has passed. Freedom can no longer survive as a lone island in a hostile sea.

CONSERVATIVE: I am afraid I don't understand the point of your argument. You say we need a foreign aid program directed to the underdeveloped world for our own protection. The fact is, we've had such a program since President Truman's Point Four proposal in 1949. After more than fifteen years, you'd think we would have something to show for our efforts. And, if our billions of dollars in aid have wrought little change, as you suggest, doesn't it occur to you that these handouts are not the answer?

LIBERAL: Our foreign aid program can boast of a number of successes since the Marshall Plan. However, most of our aid to the underdeveloped world has been military aid, and the bulk of it has been sent to Turkey, Pakistan, Vietnam, South Korea, and Nationalist China. In many cases, the amount of actual economic assistance aimed at large scale industrial development has not been adequate to do the job.

What Americans must realize is that we urgently need a Marshall Plan for the underdeveloped world. According to most estimates, a plan to make the emerging nations self-sustaining would require anywhere from two to four billion dollars a year, in strict economic aid, for a period of four to five years. This is a tiny fraction of our national income, which we could easily afford. On the other hand, the cost of inaction in this theater of the cold war could be our independence and freedom.

By this I don't mean that merely paying out several billion dollars a year will automatically transform every backward agrarian society into a dynamic industrial nation with no interest in Communist panaceas. Many nations must undergo varying degrees of political and social change before our aid can hope to reach their peoples. Simple anti-Communism is not enough. We must learn to understand the class conflicts and social upheavals sweeping these nations, different as they may be from our own middle-class values and experience, if we expect our programs to be effective. Thanks to the Communists, the incentive to learn, and learn quickly, is not lacking.

• *The United Nations is in the hands of an international gang of soft-headed neutralists who play right into Red hands.*

CONSERVATIVE: Of all the areas in the field of foreign policy, the United Nations is the most indicative of the flabby, well-meaning, but ill-conceived liberal notions on international relations. Most liberals you talk to have a kind of romantic feeling about the United Nations as some sort of international consortium of good will, an influence for world law, and an agency of reconciliation and social welfare. Well, it's not. In twenty years it has proved itself neither a constructive power for liberation nor an effective forum for peace. It's too weak to impose world law and order, but just strong enough to be a threat to our own independence. At the same time, its Secretariat is the spawning ground of international socialistic schemes and agencies and a refuge for Communist spies and infiltrators. Without adequate safeguards to our own interests, we've been plunged into a situation where our vote counts only as much as the smallest emerging nation, but where we end up footing a lion's share of the operational cost.

LIBERAL: One of the points I've been trying to stress in our discussion of foreign policy is the primary necessity to accept given world conditions as they are, not as we would like them to be, and not necessarily in the context or framework of our national experience. Once facing these realities, I think it is then possible to approach the various problems which beset us internationally, disarmed of the narrow and unrealistic slogans which constrict our activity and blur our abilities to perceive. The United Nations is a case in point.

You are correct that the United Nations is not all we would have hoped it to be; however, I think we must look at what the organization is, not what it isn't. While the United Nations may not have been powerful enough in the past to call erring nations to task for their aggressions or aberrations, it has served as a broker through which reconciliation and mediation of disputes could take place. It has provided a forum and an opportunity for exchange of views, and has succeeded in conducting affairs in a neutral and nonpartisan manner. The United Nations wasn't able, in itself, to resolve the Korean conflict or the questions of Palestine, the Congo, or Cyprus, but it has administered the ceasefires. What would any one of these situations have been like without the presence of the United Nations?

In addition to the peace-keeping functions of the United Nations, the role of its agencies is hardly as you characterized them. For instance, the International Civil Aviation Organization coordinates international air traffic control, communications, beacons, ranges, and search and rescue techniques. The International Maritime Consultative Organization has similar responsibilities in international shipping. The International Postal Union and the International Telecommunication Union are two indispensable agencies for worldwide communications.

As for the agencies which deal in the area of welfare and education, you may label them socialistic, but they are striving to eliminate those depressed areas and underprivileged conditions where Communism seems to have its greatest appeal. The International Labor Organization works to improve labor conditions and establish minimum labor standards, such as outlawing child labor. The Food and Agricultural Organization informs the farmers of the world on how to improve their crop yield, combat animal diseases, and raise nutrition levels. The World Health Organization works around the world to combat epidemics and establish uniform drug standards and accounting. The United Nations Educational, Scientific, and Cultural Organization provides worldwide educational assistance, and the United Nations Children's Fund works for the health, education, and welfare of children around the world. Now, it is true that every United States dollar is not identifiable in all these functions, nor do the people who benefit from them know to whom the credit belongs. However, I don't think that's really an issue with conservatives;

you have never really been for this kind of aid program even when we could have claimed full credit for it under our own administration.

CONSERVATIVE: The aspect of the United Nations which disturbs me the most is the possibility that a supranational organization such as this could meddle in national affairs, or eventually that it could become a world government. I wouldn't want a majority of the other countries to pass laws which would interfere with our activities. It's not inconceivable that the Communist bloc and the Afro-Asian bloc could act to force changes in racial relations here. If liberals ever succeeded in repealing the Connally Reservation, there's no telling what would happen to our system of law. Certain rights in our own Constitution might come under review by people who don't share our long tradition of freedom.

LIBERAL: Your fears of intervention in domestic affairs are unfounded. The United Nations does not have the power to enter any state without the government's permission, nor can it force a nation to change any of its laws or actions. It cannot conscript American soldiers or levy taxes on the United States. All substantive action taken by the Security Council is subject to a United States veto. The influence of the United States upon the Security Council is indicated by the fact that the United States has never found it necessary to cast a veto to stop Security Council action. Resolutions adopted by United Nations bodies other than the Security Council but including the General Assembly are in the form of recommendations and have no binding power on individual member states.

In reality, I think the basic mistrust you have for the United Nations has not yet been explicitly stated in your charges against it. I may be reading too much into your statements, but I detect a basic anxiety which seems to underlie your whole attitude toward foreign affairs; that is, namely, an unwillingness to accept the fact that, although the United States has a great influence in the world, it can by no means call all the shots. I think it's this lack of control that worries you most. Unfortunately, however, it is a fact of life we must face. Not everyone shares our values and traditions, or approves of our actions. A world of diverse systems, approaches, and traditions must be approached with a willingness to accept diversity, an appreciation for individuality among nations, and a flexibility to cope with realities. In such a world, with issues of varying complexities, we need just such an agency as the United Nations to see that every nation, both large and small, has its rights respected and its voice heard. Moreover, the United Nations provides a meeting place where misunderstandings caused by such differences in values and traditions can be examined and explained. Understanding is a basic prerequisite to peaceful relations.

6
Naïve optimism, idealism and change

Conservatives see themselves as the practical people of the world, concerned with facts, not fables. They see liberals as impractical, given to pie-in-the-sky thinking and ill-considered action. While they admit that liberalism has a certain popular appeal, conservatives believe that it contains the seeds of social and economic degeneration.

Liberals also see themselves as the practical ones; but in a somewhat different light. The facts that concern them, they say, are the facts of contemporary reality—the truths of the present, not merely the images of the past. To most liberals, present day conservatism represents little more than a rehash of obsolete social and economic thinking, and liberals feel that conservatives remain attached to a mythical condition of a world that might once have been. Within this world, conservatives react and respond to a world they can neither perceive nor accept, and before any meaningful conservative-liberal dialogue can take place, liberals believe that the conservative must be led into an acceptance of the present world with its ensuing confusion and complexities.

Until this is done, liberals believe that conservatives will continue to belabor liberal government, blaming FDR and those who followed for everything from fluoridation of water to the falling value of the dollar. To sum up this discussion we will attempt to examine these two opposing views of reality, particularly the issue of what constitutes practicality in the present age, and who holds an accurate judgment of man and his capabilities.

Particularly, we will center this discussion around the empirical realities of the present role of government, judging each viewpoint in terms of the functioning of contemporary society.

• *Liberals are too optimistic, having a sadly misplaced faith in their ability to change the basic conditions of man's existence.*

CONSERVATIVE: Before this discussion comes to a close, I think that we should go back to the basic premises of the liberal philosophy and reexamine them. This might be rather difficult for you, as most liberals seem to lack the ability to face facts. If you will bear with me, however, I will be able to show you the falsity of your present approach. Quite simply I think, liberals always seem to be much too idealistic and place far too much trust in the good nature of people. Stop and look at the world about you; see what people are. People will only work because they are afraid of hunger, not because of higher purpose, internal motivation, or some other piece of psycho-sociological tripe that liberal social scientists have manufactured to obscure the basic human shortcomings.

LIBERAL: On the contrary, we are well aware of human shortcomings; in fact most of the liberal programs that you decry are not based on any ideal sort of man, but are designed to help man in his imperfection to become somewhat more capable, and get something more out of life. We do not say that the nature of man is good as you claim we do, or essentially bad as you would like to claim. We only say that the human animal is *perfectible* —not perfect.

CONSERVATIVE: Again you show your optimistic naïveté. Let's look at slum clearance, for example. Why, if what you said was true about being able to perfect or improve defective human beings, the mere act of moving people out of slums should have helped, and should put these people on the road to a new life.

The slum dwellers mark up the walls, break the windows, wreck the pumbing, turning the apartments into slums again. I won't go so far as to say that you can't change patterns of action at all —the churches accomplish something—but I do say that you can't change it much.

LIBERAL: I'm glad you brought up housing. You're quite right to point out the naïveté of the well-intentioned people who thought slum clearance would cure slums. Today we know that improved housing is only one step, and that slum dwellers often need other kinds of help to achieve a better environment. Now let's look further. After we discovered that new housing alone didn't work, liberals set out to learn what else was needed. Although we certainly don't know all the answers yet, we've found out a lot. But the point lies in the different kinds of response which liberals and conservatives made to the discovery. The conservative responds, "Forget about public housing. The slums will be with us a long time. You can't change human nature— much." The liberal says: "Let's have more public housing. And let's see what other help slum dwellers need before slum conditions can be alleviated."

• *Liberals meddle with people's lives.*

CONSERVATIVE: But don't you see you're demonstrating the point I was trying to make? Liberals don't understand human nature. You keep trying to change the habits of those poor slum dwellers. First you try housing. That doesn't do it. Then you try Aid to Education. That doesn't do it. Then you try the War on Poverty. When will you realize that it's useless to try to manipulate people?

LIBERAL: "Manipulate"? Tell me, is it manipulation to compel children to go to school and to compel parents to send them? I suppose so. Education hasn't always been compulsory in our country. Now it is—by state law, incidentally, not federal. And all of us who have brought up children (or remember our own schooldays) know that education doesn't happen to a child spontaneously. Somebody has to provide proper education and somebody has to see that the child is systematically exposed to it. This is "manipulation" in two ways—in the immediate sense that the child and his parents are not given a choice: he has to go to school; and in the deeper sense that education is a pretty fundamental manipulation of a child's outlook. Notice that in the United States we surround the process of education with quite a few safeguards to prevent the introduction of questionable material. We try to keep our schools from being biased or manipulated for private ends. We try to encourage the child to keep an open mind. But when all is said and done, we have to admit that, in sending a child to school, society changes the child's outlook, modifies his nature.

So, call it manipulation or whatever you like, education illustrates the point which people have long since decided: that human character often *needs* certain modification and that schools could be set up to provide it. Even conservatives accept the need, if not always the means, of educating people.

CONSERVATIVE: I'm glad you are aware that conservatives aren't always happy with educational methods, especially some of the modern ones. But in switching our discussion of human nature from housing and its failures, to education . . .

LIBERAL: Weren't you going to add, "and its failures"?

CONSERVATIVE: Perhaps out of long habit I was, but that is ir-relevant. The thing I'm driving at is that liberals carry their at-tempts to manipulate human nature too far. Education, yes; housing, no.

LIBERAL: Where do you draw the line? Education, yes, you say. How about health?

CONSERVATIVE: Liberals talk in such mouth-filling categories! "Health"? Health means many things.

LIBERAL: What about maternity and infant health? Take one item: the regulation that a doctor must put a drop of silver ni-trate in each eye of every newborn baby to prevent blindness arising from syphilitic infection. Is this a good regulation?

CONSERVATIVE: There you go, reducing the argument to the ri-diculous. Of course, no one objects to common-sense health measures like that.

LIBERAL: What about tuberculosis of the bone, which created so many hunchbacks all through the centuries? We've almost eliminated this in the last few decades by wiping out certain dis-eases in cattle and hogs—through federal and state government action.

CONSERVATIVE: That makes sense, of course.

LIBERAL: Well then, what about the regulation in some states that iodine be put in all table salt to prevent goiter?

CONSERVATIVE: I suppose you're leading up to asking me about fluorine in drinking water to prevent cavities in teeth.

LIBERAL: That's right—though I really don't care at the moment what your answer is. I want to illustrate a larger point. You agree that the government—society—ought to do some things that have a profound impact on human nature, such as educating children and eliminating infection, blindness, and tuberculosis. But you aren't sure how far we should go.

CONSERVATIVE: I'm sure we should not go as far as England does, where the government provides false teeth!

LIBERAL: You're saying that you don't agree with every proposal, that some go too far, but that society—government—ought to do some of these things. This is precisely what liberals say, but I suspect that we use some different yardsticks to measure our choices. Frankly, I've always suspected conservatives of a little unconscious hypocrisy on this point. When you say that a welfare program is contrary to human nature, you don't really mean that it's contrary to the nature of the recipient of the help, but that it infringes on the human nature of the taxpayer.

CONSERVATIVE: Come on now—when you can't think of any valid argument, you accuse us of self-interest.

LIBERAL: Am I wrong?

• *Liberal   policies   damage   society   by   disturbing   normal human relations.*

CONSERVATIVE: I don't think it's self interest. We feel that when you run counter to human nature you are damaging society.

LIBERAL: You mean that liberals are hurting people by disturbing the normal human relations and setting up artificial ones?

CONSERVATIVE: Yes. You can see the results piling up year by year. Children learn that they will get through school regardless of what effort they put forth. People learn that they will be taken care of whether they exert themselves or not.

LIBERAL: Of course these things happen—in a few cases. Where classrooms are overcrowded and where children begin school with inadequate backgrounds, they get pushed along. Notice that the liberals are always trying to get more teachers and more classrooms? And now we're working on preparation problems through Operation Headstart, the program for deprived preschoolers. But these situations are the exception; there is no sign of a breakdown of motivation among students generally. And I don't see any indication of a growing body of adults who aren't motivated to get ahead, except for some young people who have been school dropouts. Incidentally, the proportion of school dropouts is going down, not up. But, as you know, the problem of what these young people can do in society is growing, since the number of unskilled jobs is not increasing at all. We are working on this too, through the Job Corps and special training programs.

Apart from these people, do you see any growing number who won't work? I think the reverse is true. We are constantly being pressed by an expanding work force. The rewards of work are so exciting, so great, and growing so fast these days that the opportunity just to subsist isn't attracting many takers.

CONSERVATIVE: You have been talking about children and unemployed teenagers. You've forgotten about the farmers who put their land into the Soil Bank and get paid for not raising anything.

LIBERAL: They get paid for the use of their land by the country just as a landlord is paid for the rent of his building. If either chooses to do no other work, we don't call him idle.

- *Liberals are too idealistic and impractical.*

CONSERVATIVE: Let's look at another point that's closely related and goes to the very heart of the difference between conservatives and liberals. You go too far in your idealism. You try to do the impossible and you don't take a good hard look at the cost. For example, the War on Poverty is going to be mostly an exercise in futility. Maybe you'll be able to do a little good here and there, but you can't wipe out poverty. We've always had the poor with us. Some people will always have trouble making a living.

LIBERAL: Some will—but fewer people all the time. Thirty-five years ago—just before the Great Depression—sixty-eight percent of our people lived below what we call the poverty level. That means an income of less than $3,000, figured in 1965 dollars or equivalent buying power, for a family of four. Today only twenty-one percent live below that level. Those that pushed above it—almost half the population—did so because they had opportunity.

There is no reason to think that a lot of the twenty-one percent can't do likewise. If we can expand their opportunity through programs like the War on Poverty, we can make it possible for a lot more of them to push over the line. Then think of the results in increased tax revenue and decreased public and private assistance. Your argument about spending only holds if we fail—if people continue to be dependent.

CONSERVATIVE: I said one of the differences between us is that incurable optimism of yours.

LIBERAL: It isn't optimism, it's common sense. If people can't grow out of their dependence through the help of their families, training, education, remedial health measures, and other means, they become a burden on all of us. If we help them take advantage of the resources of society to become self-supporting, we are freed of the burden and they gain human dignity. Considering all the facts, I think it is more correct to say that the "idealistic" liberals are more practical than the "hard-headed" conservatives. The history of our country, in fact the history of Western civilization since the Dark Ages, has been a struggle—increasingly successful—for the emergence of the individual from poverty, enslavement, and degradation to human dignity, freedom and material well-being. That struggle has always been guided by hopes and ideals; it's been aided by individuals and institutions. Sometimes government has helped; for many centuries and in many places government has been an impediment. But as democratic forces have taken over, you'll have to admit that government has been increasingly effective as an agent for improvement.

It is the conservatives who need to look at history to see that idealism—which is really another way of describing hope—has been one of the great, practical moving forces that have brought us where we are.

• *Liberal goals are impossibly utopian.*

CONSERVATIVE: Liberals have a lot more faith in getting to utopia than conservatives have. That expectation of reaching an idyllic goal, that firm belief that there is such a thing as utopia, is one of the places we think liberals go overboard.

LIBERAL: We're talking about people becoming self-supporting. What's so utopian about that?

Now I'd like to ask *you* a question. We've been skirting the subject of national goals; I'd like to see how our ideas compare on what we hope for the future of our country. How would you define conservative goals for America?

CONSERVATIVE: Individual freedom and dignity, a free society, free enterprise, decentralized government, a peaceful world.

LIBERAL: I think most liberals would agree with those goals, but we might describe them differently. Take individual freedom. From what you say, I deduce that you mean maximum freedom for those who already have freedom—as little change as possible in the present distribution of freedoms. For example, you would favor continuing the freedom of an employer to hire anyone he chooses, even though this means continuing the lack of freedom of a potential Negro employee to be hired for his ability.

CONSERVATIVE: You misunderstand me. I'm opposed to discrimination on any grounds—religion, race, or national origin.

LIBERAL: In principle, yes. But when it comes to curtailing someone's freedom of action to enforce the right, you're not so sure. You tend to say: Let those who have freedom keep it. Liberals more often define freedom as something that *everyone* ought to share; we think of it as freedom of opportunity. Conservatives tend to oppose any change in laws or restrictions; liberals try to weigh each proposal in terms of its effects, for the greater good of society: Will it create more freedom than it removes? Will it remove a great burden for some people while imposing a very moderate burden on others? Are the people from whom the burden is being removed heavily disadvantaged? Does the change in the *status quo* contribute to equality of opportunity? Notice, we don't advocate equality. We do look forward to a better distribution of opportunity.

CONSERVATIVE: That's utopia, 1984 edition.

• *How can liberals expect to preserve American principles while advocating radical change?*

LIBERAL: Your mentioning utopia is symptomatic of something I've observed about conservatives. When I talked about change, your comment was "utopia." Now I know that this was a gentle way of chiding me about my impractical ideas, but I think it revealed two more things about your approach to change. First, calling something utopian lets you dismiss it from mind with a clear conscience: the liberal approach is too "far out;" you don't have to consider it seriously. Second, and far more important: when you label change utopian, you don't have to think about possible gradations of change. Liberals believe that gradations and degrees of change are the very heart of the matter.

Change is all around us—in science and the physical world, in economics and business, in social institutions. No one can question the fact of change. The things we can effect through government to some extent are its direction and its speed. The nature of change—how it happens, what it alters, what results from it—determines which of our principles, our customs and traditions, our ways of life we can retain.

There are three broad approaches people can take to change. Some categorically oppose it, often simply from the habitual and very human fear of the unknown. Some are devoted to change for its own sake and so accept or encourage it indiscriminately. Some want to participate in it selectively.

Most liberals fall into the third group. We don't automatically say that change is good. And we are afraid of a state of mind that says that no change is good. Why? Because we don't think either is a practical way to cope with our changing world.

Government needs to recognize the constant flow of new events and to find ways to cope with the changed conditions they create. When you try to prevent all change in a given field, or offer too little, too late, you simply magnify the pressure for change and court disruption of the very thing you're trying to preserve. Each problem and each possible solution needs to be thought out on its own merits and in the light of all the relevant circumstances. When government does this effectively, the result is not the destruction of the past but the continuation and development of the past into a useful, healthy present.

CONSERVATIVE: How can you say that changing things preserves our past principles?

LIBERAL: Maybe an example or two will help. Let's go back to the first Antitrust Act, passed in 1887. It was proposed in an era when business was beginning to increase in size and to develop many devices in restraint of competition—artificial railroad rates that discriminated between competitors, rebates to certain purchasers, bribery or coercion of transportation agencies, the development of local monopolies, the beginning of great regional trusts and combines. Here was a problem that troubled both conservatives and liberals. Liberals saw that business practices were being developed which would foster monopoly and ultimately undermine the great principle of competition upon which free enterprise rests. Conservatives recognized the damage to competition, but saw government intervention as an even greater danger because they expected that regulation would supersede competition.

The restraint of trade became such a glaring evil that the liberals won the argument. Legal limits were placed upon competitive methods. Other legislation followed over the years, keeping pace with changing conditions; and regulations of the Department of Justice and interpretations by the courts have developed a great body of antitrust procedure.

What has been the result? Has private industry been weakened as the conservatives of 1887 expected? Obviously, private enterprise has flourished. In spite of the enormous size of many units of business, competition today is reasonably effective. And this healthy competition has been a great bulwark for private ownership. Few people talk any more about the "malefactors of great wealth." Business, which might have grown big and fat and oppressive, has instead grown big, somewhat lean, and reasonably mindful of public need and public principle.

Let's look at a second case, the establishment of the Federal Reserve System in 1914. Banks have always been a problem for the country, beginning in 1791 with the chartering of the Bank of the United States, in which the federal government owned some of the stock and in which all government funds were deposited. In 1832 the Bank was still under controversy; Andrew Jackson attacked it as a danger to the country's growth and freedom, and he won reelection to the presidency largely because of his opposition to it. A few years later the Bank was dissolved.

Over the years the federal government has evolved programs for chartering private banks, and the separate states have developed their own banking laws and state charters. By 1914 the banking system was working less well all the time, yet even then there were strong counsels for the government to keep hands off, to "let well enough alone." The proposal to establish the Federal Reserve System, which would require every federal bank to maintain some deposits at the Reserve and which set up procedures for expanding and contracting credit, opened up all the worries about the dangers of a government-connected central bank. Was this not the beginning of a government takeover of the banking system? At the very least, conservatives said, it would set off unpredictable meddling with banking and credit. Many people feared that this was the beginning of the end of free enterprise, the entering wedge of socialism.

But in 1914 the Federal Reserve System was established. What has happened since then? There have been periods when the Treasury has influenced Federal Reserve policy more than some people think wise. But the development of the Federal Reserve has been a spectacular example of adaptation to the country's changing needs. The Reserve has contributed to fiscal flexibility, to the growth and security of the banking system, to great stability in money and credit, and to confidence in our whole system of private enterprise.

Not all cases of federal intervention have persisted. Policies have been tried and abandoned, either because they were not successful or because their usefulness was over. Perhaps the most outstanding examples of this were our wartime control programs, such as price control, production controls, and man-power controls. Then there was the protective tariff, which is now gradually being eliminated; unlimited coinage of silver, which promoted the development of mining in the West and is no longer economically feasible; the tax on retained profits; wartime subsidies for production of minerals, and many others.

CONSERVATIVE: I am glad to see that liberals sometimes favor *removing* government regulations, not just adding more.

LIBERAL: Of course we do. The main point is that every problem and every proposed solution needs its own thorough consideration by our public servants and by each of us as citizens in a democracy.

You know, it's curious. You accuse the liberals of being impractical; but it is the conservatives who so often advocate the over-simple solution, the answer based on a single doctrinaire point of view, or on one part of the consequences. It is conservatives who so frequently oppose new ideas just because they seem to go counter to a rule or a principle, without really examining their effect. This is why liberals are inclined to regard conservatives as the dogmatic theorists of this world—not the realists after all. We invite you to join us on the proving grounds of the new ideas, the new experiments, the new solutions.

And last, a very important question: How can the conscientious citizen determine, as we hammer out the answers of the future, whether the pros or the cons are right? He can't be sure. But he can use these yardsticks: Has there been careful, deliberate discussion of the issue? Have all sides of the question been heard, including the points of view of the special interests who will be benefited or injured? Have the general interest and the special interests been weighed? Is the legislative or administrative decision being made by public servants who are representative of the electorate? Will the action be subject to court review, and can we reconsider it at a later date for possible modification or repeal?

• *How can anyone tell if this country is following the right course?*

CONSERVATIVE: You're saying that there isn't any one sure test for the rightness of government action?

LIBERAL: Yes. There is no essential guarantee that the country will do the right thing. You can't be ruled by inaction, you can't trust *a priori* rules, you can't rely on precedent or tradition, you can't rest on the Constitution, you can't fall back on "human nature" or "natural law," you can't even prove your point with Scripture. All of these things enter into any conclusion that is reached. But the decisions themselves must rest upon human judgment, rising out of an examination of all the relevant facts. In a democratic society there is no ultimate guardian, no source of authority, beyond our own collective judgment.

What could be a greater inducement to the development of wisdom, of understanding, of all those qualities of good sense and mutual respect which make a nation great, than this magnificent responsibility to govern ourselves with care, patience, and the courage to dare?

What greater challenge can we face?